MW00974146

# READY, FIRE, AIM

## A Relentless Pursuit to Find Sustainable Joy

PHILIP FLOOR

WESTBOW
PRESS®
A DIVISION OF THOMAS NELSON
& ZONDERVAN

WestBow Press books may be ordered through booksellers or by contacting:

WestBow Press
A Division of Thomas Nelson & Zondervan
1663 Liberty Drive
Bloomington, IN 47403
www.westbowpress.com
1 (866) 928-1240

ISBN: 978-1-9736-4851-2 (sc)
ISBN: 978-1-9736-4853-6 (hc)
ISBN: 978-1-9736-4852-9 (e)

Library of Congress Control Number: 2018914741

Print information available on the last page.

WestBow Press rev. date: 01/09/2019

*To those closest to us who have wandered so far from Him, may this book lead you back.*

# CONTENTS

# A LETTER TO MY READERS

I want to start off by telling you what my intentions aren't. I am not trying to get you to go to my church or say you can only experience the things I am going to share in a church like mine. I am not trying to convert you to any type of beliefs. I am not asking you to abandon any specific things or lifestyles. I am not trying to say you have to do what I did to get to where I got. I am not trying to do any of those things.

What I am trying to do is give you insight into what a year can look like. I want to give you insight into what a sense of community and belonging can feel like. I'd like to show what simply jumping in, saying yes, and asking questions later can result in. I'd like to show another option to the way things are done and life is lived. I want the best for you, and I am simply offering some suggestions to ponder. What you decide to do at the end of it all is your business.

So often in life when a decision needs to be made on whether to do something or not, we analyze the pros and cons, think of the outcomes, contemplate the time it will take, and seek an understanding of why we should or shouldn't do something. Those are all great methods to smart decision-making. Without those steps, many things could go south, people could get hurt, and lives could be negatively affected forever.

These stories I am going to share go 100 percent against everything I just said in the previous paragraph. The things I did, the decisions I made, and the experiences I had were not calculated. They were not thought out. Pros and cons weren't weighed. Asking the question "Why?" just didn't happen. Instead I took the stance of "Why not?" I jumped fully into everything that came my way. I decided, for once in my life, I'm going to completely say yes and not stop until I discover enough reasons to. I was tired of asking questions and never actually taking a step. Instead for one year, I said yes and figured I'd ask questions later.

This book is comprised of chapters that each contains an individual journey I experienced while attending a church and getting involved in a community for one entire year. This journey is not one everyone goes on, and people who do go can experience a multitude of outcomes. This is simply my journey—one through my first year actively following Jesus in the local church.

The starting line was one of broken faith and hatred. The finish line is one of full-hearted following of Jesus and passion for the local church. All along the way, I want to point out the impact the local church can have in one's life, how God perfectly orchestrates our lives, and how there isn't a single event we experience that God can't use for His glory.

These stories will take you on a roller-coaster ride of wonder, disbelief, heartbreak, suffering, and finally pure joy. I will do my best to tell these stories in the order that they happened; however, some start simultaneously and end at different times while others commence at different times but end simultaneously.

To help you along while reading this book, think of each chapter as one systematic theme taking place over the course of the year. Each theme is comprised of various short stories, all strung together to create a full picture of what the year looked like through the theme.

Throughout the stories, you will see where I inserted excerpts of journal entries I made both during the time these events were taking place and after they occurred where I reflected on them. These entries are provided to help give insight into the thoughts going on inside of me, the changes forming, and the understandings I was gaining. Don't allow the dates of the entries to confuse you on the timeline of events. I do my best to explain whether the entry was written during the time or as a reflection of the time at a later date.

One other thing you will find in your journey through these stories is at the end of each chapter where I break away from the story to share some things I learned, wisdom passed on, and helpful tidbits I collected along the way. These things all apply way outside of the context of the lens of faith and the local church, and I hope they help you, your understandings, and your overall growth in life as much as they helped me.

I can only hope through all of these stories, one of them will stand out to you or cause you to think deeper, reflect, and ultimately take your step closer to God. My end goal is simple. I'll come right out and say it so there aren't any surprises. My hope is, through these stories, you would consider giving the local church another try.

There are so many reasons in today's society where people have walked out of the church forever, and most of those motives are probably valid. I've heard so many stories where I have said, "Yup, I would have left too." I don't want to dismiss any of those reasons as to why you left in the first place. What I do want is to show you what the church can be, why so many people choose to invest in it, and what could be possible if you were to turn back and walk in one more time.

Now, if you are reading this and are already in church or swear you would never go again, please keep reading. I promise there are so many things through these stories that can benefit and help you along the way through your journey of life. Hopefully you will discover the endless opportunities available by simply saying yes when so often we say no and how simple perspective shifts can open up a whole world that has never been discovered. I'm praying for each and every one of you throughout your journey in these stories.

I have one final thing before we dive in, some promises. I

promise to be honest, real, raw, and vulnerable when telling these stories. Too often we read and hear these superficial stories where everything goes right, nothing goes wrong, and the person in the story has a perfect past.

Well, my past is so far from perfect, not everything turned out the way I thought it would, and not every story has a fairy-tale ending. I did my very best to give as much context as possible to all of these stories to point out a timeline of the life I once lived and how it was transformed.

By no means do I want to portray my life as being better than anyone else's. In no way do I want to come off sounding boastful or bragging. I have tried my best to write with the upmost humility. My story is not an isolated incident. Thousands of people have tales just like mine. I just decided to write mine down and compile it into this book.

I hope you enjoy reading these stories as much as I have enjoyed living them and now writing them down.

# PROLOGUE

There seems to be a search for something in many people's lives. When we interact with people, engage in conversations, and carry out life's duties, there seems to be this endless look on the horizon to fill a void. What this is exactly seems to be different for each person. Some people are looking for fame; others are searching for purpose. A job hunt for one person can be a search for companionship for another. Someone can be looking to discover his or her identity; another can be seeking his or her purpose in life. Whatever it might be, most of us are looking, and we will not stop the search until we find what it is.

Even though people's searches might seem different, once the layers are pulled back, there is usually a commonality found amongst each one. As each journey unfolds, no matter where the path leads, the driving force is often the same. In each occurrence of a search through life, most of us are looking for one thing—a thing so powerful, fulfilling, and never ending that we tend to be lost without it. This thing is joy.

Now when I look up the word *joy*, the definition provided is "the emotion evoked by well-being, success, good fortune, or the prospect of possessing what one desires." If you're looking at the root of most people's search, one of those descriptors in the definition of joy can be found. No one actually wants the specific job, person, or understanding. People search after the things they do to fill the empty feeling. We all believe each thing we are searching for will bring us that feeling of success, good fortune, or well-being. The thing we are searching for will bring us ultimate and sustaining joy.

In my life, I have searched for joy in just about everything you can imagine. I tried to be a certain person, buy specific things, hang out with particular people, and follow certain interests. The list goes on and on. Every time, I seemed to always come up short. The joy was always fleeting.

When the joy would run out, I would go running to the very next thing. Typically I was sprinting to something emptier than the thing before. I searched and searched, hoping and begging these things would be the solution to the emptiness inside, the answer to the joy I so longed for, but I was left disappointed every time.

Finally, after years and years of destruction in my life, mostly self-inflicted, I found the answer. I discovered the key that unlocks the thing that filled the void inside of me, the space, I believe, inside all of us. If filled with this particular thing, it will bring us everlasting joy and fulfillment. The thing I found was Jesus, and I found Him in the local church.

## The Shooter or the Bullet

When I was in college, I had a friend named James, whom I hung out with a lot. We were in the same fraternity together, and man, did we have our fair share of fun and shenanigans. Most of the time, none of our adventures were planned. Our lives were simply being lived by doing whatever whenever. I will go ahead and say that this wasn't the most responsible way to live, but it definitely was never a dull way to exist.

Throughout all of these adventures, we ended up in some pretty well—let's just say—interesting situations. Some were hilarious. At least we thought so. However, looking back on them now, I am surprised I'm here today writing to you. Every time we would end up in one of our situations, we always had a saying.

James and I would say, "It seems like we live our lives *ready, fire, aim.*"

Then we would laugh uncontrollably. It always lasted longer than it should because James' laugh was amazingly hilarious.

*Ready, fire, aim* was how we decided we were ready to do something. We simply started doing it. One could say we pretty much set ourselves up for failure every single time. However, it definitely left us with a few stories along the way.

As we continued through college, graduated, and very slowly started maturing, we stopped having our "ready, fire, aim" adventures. This opened up some time for me to actually think about what the phrase means and why we felt it applied so much to us.

When someone is setting up to shoot a target with a gun, multiple things need to be calculated before pulling the trigger. First, assess the environment and target. Then check your stance and grip. Following this, point the gun in the appropriate direction. Finally when everything is ready, pull the trigger, trusting everything was done properly for the bullet to hit the target. This process has always been described as "ready, aim, fire."

James and I had it all wrong. We would grab the gun, fire the bullet, and then try to figure out where it was going. I haven't done a lot of shooting, but I can't imagine after the bullet is fired, one is able to control where it goes. This was the mentality we lived by though.

Following college, the mentality changed. As I entered the real world and started dealing with various problems, I stopped the "ready, fire, aim" mentality. The new thing I started doing was the absolute opposite way to how I always lived.

Before doing anything, I started carefully planning it, weighing every option, and finally pulling the trigger if everything checked out ok. This worked great for a while and provided me with the much-needed feeling of control over what I was doing, how I was doing it, and in what way the outcomes would happen.

I realized though with this lifestyle being applied to every aspect of my life, I was limiting myself on so many fronts. I was eliminating the element of hope and faith from my life. There were so many things I never did because I couldn't completely calculate all the risks and outcomes as well as completely control what would happen. Anytime I had to have hope or faith that things would turn out for the best, I would simply stop aiming the gun and put it down. This put my life in a box.

At times, friends would ask me to go places I had never been to before or do activities I had never done before that I turned down simply because I couldn't calculate all the outcomes and risks. This caused me to miss out on so many fun things. Other times when I wanted to try something new that had the potential to be a healthy replacement of certain things I was doing in my life, I resisted because I didn't know if they would actually help and was intimidated by stepping into an unfamiliar territory without the promise that things would work out for the better.

As one could imagine, eventually I got tired of this lifestyle. I was tired of limiting my life, my situations, the people I would engage with, and the results that could happen because I was afraid to take risks, having the fear of not being able to control the outcomes and knowing things wouldn't work out how I calculated them.

With this frustration of how things have been in my life, I decided to revisit the phrase James and I lived by a few years earlier but look at it in a different way. Instead of being the careless shooter who just fired the bullet and tried aiming where it would go after, I decided to be the bullet and allow someone or something else to be the shooter. For one year, I decided to give God a chance through the local church, to allow Him to be my shooter, to aim where I go, and to control when I was fired.

I had no idea what I was getting into and couldn't have imagined all that was to happen, but it didn't matter to me. I no longer wanted to be in control of a life that had become so little. I wanted to find the joy I so longed for. So I took the biggest risk I would ever take. I turned the control over to God as my shooter and I His bullet.

Join me as I journey you through what that year looked like. Ready, fire, aim!

# CHAPTER 1
# Lonely But Not Alone

The 2016–2017 school year had begun. I was entering my third year as an elementary teacher and was eager to see what this year was going to be like. My previous two years had been nothing short of interesting, and this new year brought the hope that I would finally have at least one good year of teaching experience.

As I was sitting down to have lunch one day, my partner teacher, Heather, struck up a personal conversation with me. This was a little out of the norm for us since we had been working together for only a few weeks and hadn't gotten to know each other well yet. The topic she chose to discuss was my dating life since I was single at the time.

Heather started asking me the usual questions of how dating was going, and I gave the standard responses of how it was nonexistent. Many years had gone by since I had dated someone, and people found it odd I had been single for so long.

Heather caught on to this suspicion. "What are you doing to try to meet girls?"

I reflected on all of my pathetic attempts and explained a few. Listening intently, she processed what I said and then turned the conversation away from girls. She asked about my friends. Specifically she asked what we did on the weekends. This caught me by surprise since us teachers had never really talked about what we did outside school.

I reflected on the question for a little bit before answering, realizing what I did on the weekend was pretty much the same as my dating life. It was nonexistent. This was accompanied by the nonexistent friends I had. Aside from my roommate, just about all my friends were either still in college or out of touch.

I guess I hadn't really realized I was pretty much alone. I had wrapped myself so much into my teaching career that I had completely neglected my personal life. It seemed, along with my searches and failures of finding a girl, I was also searching and failing at finding friends without even knowing it.

I proceeded to answer Heather, explaining I kind of just hung out on the couch by myself and wrote lesson plans for the upcoming week. This led our conversation to her telling me that she might be able to help. I didn't know how she was going to assist in these departments. The little bit I had learned about her up to this point didn't seem enough to constitute helping me out.

She had only a college-aged son, so she couldn't be setting me up with a daughter or connecting me with her son's group of friends. It didn't really make much sense as to how she would help, but I said, "Sure. I'll play along."

There were only three minutes left before we had to get our students anyway, and I just couldn't stomach another bite of the interesting food I was eating from the cafeteria.

She told me there was a place where her friend's son attended a gathering on Sunday nights. She described it as a place where people my age (mid-twenties) hung out. They had bonfires, played outdoor games like cornhole, had food trucks, and listened to live music. She thought this could be a great place for me to meet some friends and have something to do on the weekends.

I don't know anyone who wouldn't be interested in all of those things. I wanted to know where this magical gathering was.

Then she said the next sentence. "They also talk about God there."

"Hold up! You can go ahead and stop right there," I said. "This is a church? I left that a long time ago. I have had many people try to get me to church, and I'm just not having it."

At that moment, what seemed so surreal turned into the unreal for me. I was completely checked out of the conversation as I looked down at my watch to see there was only one minute left before I had to get my students. And I hadn't gone to the bathroom. If I didn't go right then, I was pretty much holding it until 3:00 p.m.

As I quickly got up to go to the bathroom, Heather said the next line that changed everything. "I hear there are a lot of pretty girls there."

My body stopped in an instant as my bottom regained contact with the chair. The once completely lost attention was now fully focused like I was a fighter pilot. I only said two words following the statement. "I'm listening."

She said she had heard there were a lot of pretty girls there. And since I really didn't want to go out to the bars and such to meet girls, this might be a great option. She suggested, with all the other stuff that was going on, I could probably just ignore all the God and churchy talk. She said I could just look for girls to talk with as well as potential friends to mingle with. It sounded like a pretty sweet idea. I was definitely considering it.

The only thing that was still holding me back was the church thing. I pondered the thoughts a little more and decided it sounded great, but no thanks. This was a little too far off for me. I couldn't get past the church aspect.

So not to be rude to Heather for trying to help, I said it all sounded really great and I would definitely consider it, even though I knew it wasn't going to happen. I'd had too many bad experiences with church and wasn't about to go down that road again.

Unfortunately, I missed my bathroom window, and it was time to head back to the zoo of a cafeteria to get my students. I guess I was just going to hold my bladder and hope I didn't need to make a visit to the doctor later. The conversation with Heather was great, especially compared with the usual teacher talk we had during lunch, but I planned on never thinking about it again.

## Defenseless

A few days had passed since the conversation with Heather. I found myself doing my mind-numbing weekend routine of sitting on the couch with a TV show on, papers I just graded on the floor, and my work laptop about to be closed after writing lesson plans for the past few hours. I don't know what your mid-twenties are or were like, but as you can see by my experiences, I was living the dream!

It was mid-Sunday, and I started reflecting on my nonexistent weekend for the millionth weekend in a row. Much like my routine of TV and schoolwork, my emotional routine was pretty consistent on the weekends. I would think everything was okay and display a sense of pride for having all my work done as I headed into the new week. Then I would feel a sense of waste as I realized I had worked the entire time instead of experiencing any days off. After the sense of waste, I would scroll through my phone to see who I could text or call. I noticed, besides my mom, I pretty much wasn't in touch with anybody. This brought on the unavoidable feelings of loneliness and worthlessness.

Every once in a while, I would change it up by scrolling through one of the many dating apps on my phone, alongside some social media apps, to see if there were any girls I could be talking to. I probably don't have to lay out the conclusion for you, but just in case you are still calculating the results, it led to a whole lot of nothing.

After doing my emotional loneliness dance that particular Sunday night, I had a thought. This was a new notion in my routine, so it took me by surprise. I thought of the conversation with Heather a few days prior. Each part of the discussion replayed in my head like I was watching an old movie frame by frame. As each frame would come up, I would study its contents entirely before moving on to the next frame and repeating the process.

I must have replayed the film in my head at least two or three times. This was not a conversation I planned on revisiting so I tried as hard as I could to get it out of my head. No matter what I did to try to dismiss the thoughts though, they were almost engraved in my brain. I tried to use all my usual tactics to get out of considering doing something. *It's a church. I am too tired. I have work tomorrow. No one will go with me. I don't know anyone there. There is no point in me going anyway. I haven't had any luck before.* There was no hope of getting the conversation from my mind.

Every time I tried using one of those phrases, I kept getting the opposing thought in my head. *It's a church. So? I'm too tired. So? I have to work tomorrow. So? No one will go with me. So? I don't know anyone there. So?* Each "so" that came up left me in a state of defenselessness because I couldn't find a good response.

Due to not being able to get the thoughts out of my head with my usual tactics, I decided I would search online about this gathering and gain at least one excuse as to why I shouldn't go. I knew it was a church, so I was sure I could find some crazy, radical practices or beliefs they follow that would instantly say to me, "Yea, they are definitely a cult. I am not about to do that." Even if I couldn't find anything on that front, I was sure of a million other things I could find that would steer me away.

Nada. Nothing. I couldn't find anything. Now I'm not saying I couldn't find anything that would give me a reason not to go. I mean I couldn't really find anything on this gathering. All I could find was their website that had some vague information about what it was, a story or two that hadn't been updated in quite some time, and the address where it was located.

On any other day of the week, the lack of information would have been just what I needed to head for the hills. But for some reason, I found both my feet planted. I wasn't running. I was gazing at the site over and over again. It had almost become a mystery that I needed to solve. I needed proof as to why I didn't need to go, and I simply couldn't find any.

I thought more about Heather and my conversation. My mind was in a wrestling match. One thought in my head said, *Forget it*, while the other said, *So?* I kept thinking about the things Heather had said that sounded like such fun things to do: cornhole, live music, food trucks, pretty girls, and people in general. I went on to think about how what I currently was doing wasn't working and how I was about due for a change in scenery.

It was like a ping-pong match in my mind because I wanted to focus on all the reasons I shouldn't do it, but all the reasons I should were taking hold. That is what my life had become. Thinking of all the reasons I shouldn't do something was the norm. Anything I could use to keep me in my comfortable little bubble was what I wanted.

After much deliberation, the defining thoughts came into my mind. I always focused on the "Why not?" in my life, and it had led me to where I currently was—alone, depressed, and overworked. All I ever wanted was the absolute opposite of what I was getting. Then I remembered someone once tell me the definition of insanity was doing the same thing over and over again and expecting different results.

It was like the room got brighter and my eyes got wider. I realized I was doing the same routines over and over and expecting the friends to just come walking into the apartment, the girlfriend to come and sit down right next to me, and the loneliness to skip on out of the room, never to be seen again. Well, if the definition had any truth to it, I saw that I had to do something different.

I decided, instead of focusing on all the reasons "Why not?" like I had for so many years, I would for once just focus on all the reasons why. It was a little thought that carried a massive blow.

Next thing I know, I found myself putting down the laptop, turning off the TV, and walking toward my room to pick out something to wear. I grabbed my keys and texted my roommate that I would be back later, and off I was on a journey I never knew there would be no coming back from.

## The Last Seat

As I walked in, it was dimly lit. Rows of chairs were everywhere, and the aisles led up to a stage that had a drum set and some microphones on it. A musician my whole life, I was now deeply interested in what was going on.

I continued to look around and saw people gathered around together, socializing. To my left, I saw this huge banner that said "Come As You Are." I thought it was pretty cool because I hadn't been in many environments lately where that was openly advertised. It felt like it was more "Come If You Are," so it was refreshing to see the opposite.

My gaze continued to my left, past the banner, to see a few stations set up with some drinks that looked like you could pour yourself. I headed over to grab a drink because I saw they were serving cucumber water, which is my favorite.

Walking up to the water jug, this girl with the most infectious smile greeted me and said in the happiest voice, "Hey, I'm Leia! Welcome! I'm so glad you are here!"

My mood of investigation instantly turned upbeat as I responded, "Hey, Leia. I'm Philip. Thanks so much." I didn't necessarily know yet if I were excited to be there, but I was starting to come around to the idea. I grabbed my cucumber water and started to look for a seat.

I didn't know if I would stay the whole time, and I wanted to be prepared to make a run for it if I got too anxious to be there, so I decided I would sit in the back. I chose the last seat in the last row. I sat down and waited for it to start.

As I waited, I remembered what Heather had said about

looking for pretty girls, so searching is exactly what I did. Looking to my right, I saw one or two, and then to my left, I saw a few more. Then straight ahead, I saw some more. It seemed the odds were definitely in my favor of being able to talk to at least one.

My focus on all these pretty girls was broken as someone got up onstage and began welcoming everyone. He said, "I want to welcome you all. My name is Adam. This is a place for the young and the young at heart to experience the love of God. We are going to sing some songs and then continue our series called 'White Noise.' Why don't you say hi to someone next to you? Then go ahead and stand up, and we will get started. If you don't want to say hi to someone, just pretend to look at your phone as if you just got a text."

There was so much in the intro that I was trying to wrap my mind around and compare to what Heather had described to me earlier in the week that didn't quite add up. I felt my feet start to charge up as if I were about to make a run for the door. I looked to my left to see a couple sitting a few seats over. Somehow their gaze stopped me in my tracks, and I was able to mutter the word *hey* to them.

I began to stand up and look at the door, mapping my escape in the process. Then the first guitar chords started playing. My mind was instantly taken off my plans to escape and glued to the stage. It was one of the most beautiful things I had ever heard, and I wanted to hear more.

The song continued to play as lyrics began to scroll on the screen. I looked around as people started singing. I thought, *I am not singing!* However, I did keep listening to the song as it went from the first verse, to the chorus, to the second verse, and then back to the chorus.

My feet, once trembling in anxiety and preparing to make a run for it, were now tapping along to the beat. The bridge came up in the song as I really started listening to what the lyrics were saying.

"I won't let the storm weather my heart. Won't let the darkness beat me down. Sing in the night. My hope alive in you."

My mind started opening up as I was making connections to the darkness I was crawling out of. Just a few months earlier, I had lost my grandfather unexpectedly. The pain and confusion I felt during the time started dwelling in my mind.

Alongside the pain, I started thinking about the loneliness, depression, and anxiety I was battling with and had been battling with for quite some time. For the first time, instead of looking at it all as a pain I couldn't bear, I was looking at it as something that couldn't and wouldn't break me. A word entered my mind right there that took the place of all the words that guided me before. This was a word I hadn't thought of for quite some time. The word was *hope*.

The bridge continued. "I'll walk through the fire and not be burned. Pray in the fight and watch it turn. Jesus, tonight I give it all to you."

More and more thoughts flooded my mind. All the pain I had felt and all the weakness I had carried was now being displayed in front of me like an art collection for me to observe.

The bridge repeated itself. I started to sing. Over and over again, it repeated itself. Each time it repeated itself, I began to sing a little louder. Louder and louder I sang until I was the only one I could hear. As I sang, the pain I was feeling was turning into strength that was unshaken, unbreakable, and unimaginable.

I kept hearing the line screaming in my head. "Jesus, tonight I give it all to you." I didn't know what it meant, but I definitely knew I wasn't trying to dismiss it like all the past times in my life.

As the song ended, I started reflecting on everything that just happened. It was like nothing I had ever experienced before. It was as if my whole life were being cracked open like an egg as I watched all the contents pour out.

I can't even remember the next song that played because I was still in awe of the first. It was as if I were stunned for a moment in time. I just stood there as the song finished up, not being able to move as we prayed. Except for mine, everyone's eyes were closed and heads were bowed. Each time I tried to close my eyes, they blasted open as I continued to process what was going on inside of me.

Adam got back up on stage and stated we could all be seated and we were going to kick off the next part of the series called "White Noise."

**The Right Place**

Two chairs appeared onstage just inside two spotlights as a guy and girl sat on them. The girl introduced herself as Mallory and the guy as Joseph as she gave a recap of the series. I don't remember hearing much of the first part of the explanation as my mind finally regained consciousness, and I remembered Heather telling me this was a church.

Instantly the dramatic moment that took place in the previous song was gone as a wall went up in my mind. This was where all the "churchy" stuff was about to take place, and I was not about to listen to it. I'd heard it all before, and it didn't interest me. I was just going to continue my search for a girl to talk to after this was all over.

My search went on, row after row, girl after girl. Each aisle I scanned brought at least one person I could consider talking to. Even though my eyes were gazing the rows, my ears were apparently still focused on the stage as I heard Mallory describe what they were going to be talking about that night, loneliness.

All gazing came to a screeching halt as I refocused my eyes directly to the stage. *Loneliness?* I thought. *Loneliness? Are you kidding me? What's going on here?* I couldn't believe what was happening. The wall that shot up in my mind started coming down again as my life started pouring out in front of me.

My complete loneliness had led me there, and they happened to be talking about loneliness that very night. No matter how hard I tried to chalk it up to coincidence, I just couldn't.

*Heather just happened to tell me about this gathering the week she did? I just happened to be open-minded enough to consider going? I just happened to hit an all-time low in my loneliness journey to realize I needed to try something different? I just happened to step the farthest out of my comfort zone and walk into this place? It just happened that the song was talking about nothing breaking you? And it just happened that the message was about loneliness?* You can say all of it was coincidence, but I'm taking a different stance. I knew somehow I was supposed to be there that night.

As the message continued, Mallory told a story about a time where she battled with loneliness. She was super caught up in school and trying to make it in New York when she found herself sitting in her dorm most nights by herself. I couldn't help but think, *Hmm, that sounds familiar.*

Then Joseph went on to tell a story about his battle with loneliness. He described how to battle with the feelings and fears of loneliness. He would try to stay as busy as possible so as to make sure he was never alone or never had time to reflect on the loneliness. Eventually he realized, by making himself as busy as possible, he was making himself lonelier than ever.

*That's me! That's me!* I screamed in my head. That is exactly what I had been doing in my life up to that point. I didn't want to ever feel the loneliness that was there, so I wrapped myself in my career and various other commitments so as to not have time to ever think about the loneliness, let alone think at all. In doing so, I guess I never realized how much more lonely I was making my life.

If it weren't obvious before that I was supposed to be there, it definitely was now. I couldn't deny that my life directly resembled both of those stories. The only thoughts that were now penetrating my mind were, *What do I do now? How do I get out of this? How did they get out of this?*

I was hanging on every word being said. The next word I wasn't expecting, Jesus. *Jesus?* I thought. *How could Jesus help me with loneliness?*

To me, Jesus was someone you prayed to for some reason apparently. You celebrate His birthday on Christmas for some reason, and Easter has something to do with Him as well. How did loneliness fit into the picture of Jesus?

Then a guy named Clay came up to continue the message and explain just how Jesus could help us with our loneliness. Clay described Jesus's crucifixion and how, by dying on the cross, Jesus took the weight of all of our sin. By doing so, he actually experienced a separation from God. This separation was the ultimate loneliness one could feel, and He did it for us.

Clay explained that we deserved this separation from God, but Jesus took it for us. By doing this for us, He paved the way for us to overcome loneliness. Our hearts were meant to have an intimate relationship with God, and by Jesus dying for us, we could and can experience that intimate relationship.

Continuing on, he stated that, if you didn't know what a relationship with God looked like (which I didn't), it "is as if God is taking hold of your right hand and walking through life with you." Along with it, he explained that Jesus sent the Holy Spirit to live inside of us, causing God to never leave us. Through this, we can lean on Him in us to get through our loneliness.

Clay then posed a question for us to reflect on about our loneliness. "What if your loneliness is an invitation to lean on and absolutely connect yourself with God, allowing Him to fill you and to be aware of His presence in you? Because God in us is even more powerful than God with us."

The final takeaway from the message Clay portrayed was that we are never really alone. We might feel lonely, but we are not alone. We might experience loneliness, but we don't have to be defeated by loneliness. The best way to dig out of the deepest loneliness pit is to connect ourselves deeper with God.

My mind was completely obliterated. I didn't know what to think. I had never heard Jesus, God, or the Holy Spirit described in that way before. I never considered that God could be inside of me. I wasn't too sure about the relationship thing and leaning on Him, but I definitely liked what I heard.

All the ways I tried to battle my loneliness before seemed to only make things worse. Now, here was a way not like any other I could consider. I wasn't fully convinced of the whole church thing, but the wall I kept trying to put up in my mind to block out the churchy stuff was being destroyed time and time again as this night continued on.

## Repeat

I stood up out of my seat as the service had just ended following a prayer. There were so many thoughts running through my head that I could barely remember to breathe or blink my eyes. My mind had a slight break from all the new thoughts just long enough to remember I was there to meet girls or possibly make some friends.

Looking around the room, I tried to spot some of the girls I had my eyes on earlier. Everyone had gathered together in various friend groups, and it didn't seem like there was going to be any good opportunity for me to talk to a girl while surrounded by all her friends.

Then the search was interrupted as the first song that played when the night started began replaying in my head. I couldn't get rid of it or the accompanying thoughts that were along for the ride. I realized, even if I were able to talk to a girl, I wouldn't be able to think enough to generate a conversation. Realizing that, I decided it would be best for me to head out and try again some other time when I wasn't so distracted, if I decided to come back at all.

I walked outside and headed to my truck. Once I got in, I pulled out my phone and typed in the few lyrics I could remember from the first song that played. A search came back with the song name, "When the Fight Calls," by Hillsong Young and Free. Before I could even finish reading who had written it, I had already purchased it and downloaded it onto my phone.

I started to the play the song. Listening to more and more of the words, processing more and more areas of my life the song was revealing and speaking to, I sat motionless. The song ended.

I pressed play again. I started looking back through my past few years and all the struggles I had been through. *What was happening?* I thought. I couldn't simply make sense of anything going on. All I knew was I had to keep going and digging through my past. The song ended.

I played the song again and again and again. The routine repeated itself. More and more I thought as I dug deeper and deeper into my past. My life was playing in front of me as if it were displaying on the windshield of the truck.

Finally, after growing tired of starting the song over, I just put it on repeat. I figured I would sit there just a little longer and finish my thoughts. A little longer was an understatement.

My motionlessness started to end as I began to move along ever so slightly with the beat of the song. Little by little, my truck was filled with more than just the sound of the song as my voice started joining in. I sang and sang and sang the song over and over again.

Each time I sang the song, I became more energized, confident, and fearless than whatever I had faced and was currently facing. Louder and louder I sang as I started beating on the wheel of the truck. Tears started rolling down my cheeks as I contemplated for the first time that maybe my life had more meaning to it than I thought. All those times I felt alone, could it possibly have been that I wasn't actually alone?

Over and over again the song played, the tears ran, the beating on the steering wheel thumped, and the singing of my prideful heart sounded. Whatever was happening, I didn't ever want it to end. I couldn't help but think every once in a while, *What if I hadn't come?* Then instantly the song would start over.

Finally I looked down at the clock on the radio and saw that two hours had gone by. Looking around the parking lot, I was the only one there, and it was now dark. For two hours, I had sat and listened to the same song as I sang, cried, and contemplated my life.

I started to turn the volume down on the song as it played for the millionth time. As I turned it down, my tears began to subside. And as my tears stopped flowing, my thoughts began to settle. Now I was able to ask the question that would change my life forever, the inquiry that there was to never be any going back from. "Was Jesus with me all this time?"

Earlier in the day, I left my apartment in a swallow of loneliness. I set out to try to find some friends to cure the solitude. In reality, I set out to look for a girl to fill the void. All along the way, I tried to find any reason to turn my truck around and go back home. Nothing came up strong enough to do it.

Upon getting there, everything I thought I was looking for, the things that could cure my loneliness or at least mask it, were in attendance. People I could be friends with and girls I could mingle with all were accounted for. But little did I know, there was one person there that I wasn't after but was after me. That person was Jesus.

Here is an excerpt of a journal entry prayer I wrote later on, reflecting on the realizations I had while in the truck that night.

*11/14/16*

*Heavenly Father, My whole life I have been searching. I have been trying to fill this massive void I felt. I have tried everything I could ask for, but I still felt so disconnected and lost. I lived this alternate life in my head where I did no wrong and everyone loved me and worshipped me. This false reality I lived in my head made me so disconnected to the world and caused more pain than the pain I was covering up.*

*When I found you, Lord, I didn't need any of those things. All those things I pretended to be, you actually provided for me through your endless love. I never realized how in the dark I was until you showed me the light. I pray that I constantly have an endless thirst for you, Lord, and I continue to grow with you. Amen.*

## Words for Thought

*Loneliness*

Loneliness is one of the most soul-sucking things one can experience in life. It is the feeling that no one is there for you, no one cares for you, and no one loves you. This feeling can grow bigger and nastier as it forms into full-blown depression if it is not properly addressed.

A few weeks ago, I was talking with a friend about his loneliness and what it was doing to his life. Now this friend has a community of people around him who love him more than he could imagine.

"So why is he lonely?" you might ask.

Well, that's the worst part of loneliness. It is the feeling that people aren't there for you. I'm not a psychologist, but I'm going to go out on a limb here and say most people's loneliness, including my own, usually doesn't stem from actual physical factors like being truly alone. Usually it is this idea, this feeling, that one is alone. That is the worst part about loneliness.

A lot of times, you can't just fix it by surrounding the person with a bunch of people. In my experiences with loneliness, this would oftentimes sink in a deeper feeling of loneliness. Instead one needs to discover the root of what is causing the loneliness. Why, when so many people know, love, and want to surround someone, does he or she feel abandoned on an island? Until this reason is found, usually the person experiencing loneliness will continue to take steps back farther away from people. This soon causes the feeling to match the physical reality. Stepping far enough back, eventually the person truly is on an abandoned island alone because he or she has pushed everyone away.

This rang so true for me throughout my life, especially during my post-college years. I started battling with loneliness as my first real job came into view and I entered into the real world. During this pivotal transition period, I eventually isolated myself to the point where I was truly alone. There was no one to hang out with or talk to. I simply was waking up, going through the motions, and going back to sleep. Life seemed pretty pointless.

My life would have continued on the path of loneliness and being fully alone if something didn't change. Some kind of external or internal factor had to be altered for me to escape the soul-sucking reality of feeling I was in this all by myself.

If you find these words talking to you, something in your life has to have the same altering state for loneliness to no longer have its grasp on you. I hope through the stories in this chapter that you have found some ways to escape or avoid the prison sentence of loneliness and are able to start a new path in your journey through life. I understand if it might be hard to consider the things I have laid out in this chapter thus far, especially if it is an opposing view to yours.

*Opposing Views*

One of the most common conversations that takes place among people who are in church and those who aren't in church is the attempt to try to get those not in church to go to church. I am sure many of you have had this experience before. It can be a very worn-out conversation that oftentimes pushes you farther away. It's the constant feeling that no one is really listening to you and your problems, but instead is just trying to push his or her agenda at you. This book may have seemed like this to you.

This was my experience over and over again. The second Heather brought up church, I was heading for the hills. Something ironic is in this moment though. Often when we are dismissing people's attempts at trying to get us to go to church, we use the defense that they are not listening to us as well as all the reasons we don't want to go and aren't interested.

By us dismissing what they are saying, aren't we technically doing the same thing to them? By pushing them away and what they have to say, we are not giving the very respect and attention to what they have to say that we are expecting from them.

Along with this, we often want those people to be open-minded to our views, opinions, and reasons as to why we don't want to go to church or don't go to church. In a lot of our experiences, it seems those people didn't have the open mind. However, those people want us to come with an open mind to their views, opinions, and reasons why to go to church. If we are to be completely honest, we usually aren't as well.

This holds true for endless situations outside of the church conversation as well. When finding yourself caught in a conversation like this, regardless of either side that you are on, in church or not in church, for or against something, think about what might happen if you were to fully listen to what the other person has to say, not to just hear the sounds he or she is making with his or her mouth. But listen, process, and consider the words the person is saying to you because not listening can have consequences.

Brené Brown points out in her book *Braving the Wilderness* that we are more likely nowadays to live and exist around people who are like-minded to us than ever before. She also goes on to say, "In 1980 approximately 20 percent of Americans reported feeling lonely. Today, it's more than double that percentage. And this is not just a local issue. Rates of loneliness are rapidly increasing in countries around the world." She makes the connection that, as we live around more people who are like-minded to us, the rate of loneliness increases.

Starting to consider what the other person, the one who is bringing something to the conversation we don't agree with or want to hear, is saying can become a huge benefit to us. You might just be surprised at the sustainable joy that comes to your life and what new thing you discover or learn by doing this. Imagine what change can happen in your life if you considered what the other person says or is offering.

This, for sure, happened to me. I decided to reconsider for the first time what an opposing view on church had to say, and it ended up being the thing that changed my life forever. It can be tough to break out of what you are used to and try to consider a different way of doing things though. Doing this usually means breaking a habit or routine that has been engraved in your life and engrained in your being.

*Habits and Routines*

Getting into comfortable routines and forming habits can be very beneficial. Building habits around things, especially the miniscule tasks that we find ourselves doing every single day, can help to keep our mind from being cluttered, allow creativity to flourish, and bring our overall stress levels down. However, we don't just create routines and habits for the healthy things in our lives. In fact, I am going to go out on another limb here and say some of the hardest routines or habits to create in our lives are the healthy ones.

Exercising more, eating better, and sleeping longer are all habits that can be some of the healthiest things for us to implement in our lives but the hardest to create. The unhealthy habits, on the other hand, are easy to form, more detrimental to our life, and very hard to get out of. The addiction, the gossip, and the overworking are things very present in many of our lives and in the lives around us but are so hard to stop because they have become so comfortable and so "normal" to our way of life.

The habit that formed for me was isolation. Secluding myself in my apartment each and every weekend while continuing to work became my "normal" and the thing most comfortable for me. A lot of us tend to cling to this habit as we watch on through endless hours of social media apps and binge-watching TV shows. But the world is passing us by.

These habits oftentimes are the root to the struggles present in our lives. For example, I struggled for years with heartburn. My doctor told me to shed a few pounds, and surprisingly it went away. The habit I formed of overeating and eating super unhealthy was the main root I had to a major struggle in my life. Once I changed my habit, the impact of my struggle changed as well.

If struggles are present in your life and all the things you have tried to do to battle those toils have failed, consider looking at the habits and routines that have formed. You might just be surprised at what you find. It is easy to look for all the reasons why you shouldn't change your habits; however, those are just solidifying reasons of how you will stay exactly where you are.

I discovered after looking through what had become my normal weekend routine that nothing in my life was going to change or get better until I changed what I was doing. After you analyze those habits that might be causing struggles in your life, consider changing them, working on them, or completely obliterating them. This can take you one step closer to sustainable joy in your life.

That is what I did one Sunday night for just one time, and I never returned to the life I had again. Imagine what could happen in your life if you did the same. That very consideration requires one thing—hope.

*Hope*

Hope is a powerful word. Our abilities to overcome unexplainable odds can oftentimes be credited to the amount of hope we have that we will make it through. On the other hand, the digression and demise of our circumstances can be a result of the hope we lack, the thought we have that things will never get better. This lack of hope sways us into the viewpoint that our lives will always be what they are.

I have met with many people over coffees, breakfasts, lunches, and dinners who have shared their current struggles and the adversities put in their life's path. One thing has always reigned consistent with each person on his or her ability to have his or her circumstances turn around. The amount of hope that there was a way things could change was the consistent, deciding factor in his or her progress and the ability of his or her circumstances to change.

People who sat on the other side of the table pointing out all their problems, counteracting every piece of hope I threw at them with more and more problems, and being completely closed off that there seemed to be nothing that could be done had nothing done in their circumstances. Living in the constant negative only kept them in a negative. Nothing I said provided any change in their situations because they lacked hope.

Just last night I heard a friend talking with someone he knew on the phone as she poured out all her problems. I felt so bad for him because every attempt he tried to provide hope for her was met with instant negativity. Walking away, I thought to myself, *He will try and try to help her, but until she has hope that things can change, nothing will change for her.*

Don't allow hope to lay absent in your life. Your craziest circumstances can be battled and overcome with the start of hope in your mind and heart. Now hear me correctly. Simply hoping things to get better won't make them better. However, it will soften your mind and heart to allow in the changes needed and the approaches to take to pull you out of what you are facing.

Sitting in the last seat, I had no hope on just about every front. There was no hope that I was ever going to fix my loneliness, overcome the depressive state I had allowed myself to get in, and face the ugly battles that were weighing in on me each and every day. I was just in the room because I couldn't find a good enough reason not to be.

With the assistance from some very well written words being sung out, my mind started to open to the hope that could be. I started to pause all the negative thoughts that had held my mind captive and made room for some positive ones to work their way in. Forever grateful am I for the hope that entered my mind in the moment because it bridged the way for what was to come next. Imagine what things can come next in your life with a little more hope applied to it. I understand though if you are skeptical.

*Walls*

While reading this chapter, you might have had moments where you and many readers go while reading a Christian book. The thought usually is something like, *Here we go. I was wondering when all the Christian, churchy stuff was coming. I don't want to listen to any of this, this nonpractical nonsense.*

If this is you, I get it. I have felt this way by many books and conversations I have had in my life. Everything seems to be going great, practical information is being presented, and then bam! Here is Jesus.

This scenario I just described can be known as a Jesus juke. It is when normal conversation is happening, and then out of nowhere, the person slips in Jesus. I would say scenarios like these have turned more people away from Christianity and the church than most other reasons. It's almost as if the whole conversation were a setup for the person to get you comfortable enough to reveal his or her true intentions of why he or she is addressing you.

It would make sense after many occurrences like this why one would have a wall up, blocking out Jesus all together. Even outside the context of Jesus, moments like this happen where people get you comfortable and then sneak in their main agenda. The walls we create as a result from these events are there to protect us from these attacks and being bombarded with things that come off as nonsense.

That is how I felt that night. I knew they were going to be talking about Jesus, being a church and all, so I walked in with the biggest wall enclosing my mind and thoughts so I wasn't going to be affected by any of it. As the night went on, I started getting comfortable because it didn't seem like much churchy stuff was being mentioned, causing my wall to slowly come down. And then bam! Here is Jesus.

This caused my wall to shoot back up as I blocked out what they were saying. With my ears still listening, however, the things I was hearing didn't necessarily make sense, but they definitely made me curious. As I had stated, I never heard things explained like that before. So I started to remove my wall to explore more into what was being said.

That is what I want for you, going on from this point in the book. There will be many more Jesus juke moments throughout this book, so I want you to keep your wall up. Yes, you read that right. Go ahead and keep your wall up. However, I want you to allow your eyes and mind to continue to process the words on the pages. If things come your way that are a little different than have been presented before to you, I'd love it, if for just one moment, you removed your wall and explored more. If you don't like what you find, go ahead and put the wall back up and keep moving through. There is still so much in here for you.

I did this very process at this same point in my journey, and it set me up to slowly start seeing what had been right in front of me or, should I say, beside me this whole time. Imagine what it could be for you.

*Challenge*

Regardless of whether you are already in church, are ever going to walk back into a church, or walk into one for the first time, think about the points made throughout this journey. Imagine what new ideas you can discover and changes to the way you have always done things can be made by simply seeking out those conversations you don't want to have with those people you don't agree with.

Envision the habits that have guarded your life into a box and need so bad to be opened. By simply breaking those old habits and searching for new ones, consider what possibilities can arise. Expecting things to change, without being willing to change, will result in no change because nothing changed. I'll say that again. Expecting things to change, without being willing to change, will result in no change because nothing changed.

Keep the wall up only until you come across something different than how things have always been for you. Then for just a second, remove the wall so you can analyze the possibilities of what could be. If you don't disagree with what you find, keep the wall down as you move forward. If you do disagree, put the wall back up, but still continue to move forward in your search.

Search for the hope inside of you as you move through the days of your life. You can't hope things and all of a sudden, poof, things are better. However, you might be surprised what you are exposed to and open about when you simply enter your situation with a hopeful mind-set.

Hope is what I have for each and every one of you reading this as I finish up this chapter. I have hope that, wherever you are in your life's journey, you never face the loneliness I faced for so long. I have hope that you would consider Jesus and the church as a way out of the circumstances you might be in. I have hope that you will continue to experience the wonders and wisdom of this life as you continue reading through the stories of my life. I have hope for you.

I have told this story hundreds and hundreds of times about my first experience walking back into the church to give it another try. The same question comes up every single time I tell it, regardless of who I tell it to.

"Did you ever meet the girl?"

Every time I am asked this question, I get the biggest smile on my face. This grin is one that nothing else can quite recreate. This smile is a trigger to the memory, the starting point of everything. Following this beam, I get to answer my favorite answer of all time.

"I didn't meet the girl, but I did for the first time truly meet Jesus."

# CHAPTER 2
# I Am Jacob

Sunday after Sunday, I found myself going back to the gathering. Something was drawing me back there. What was happening inside of me, even though I wasn't quite sure what it was, made me hungry for more. I started to see change in other areas of my life as well. I was waking up happier, moving around the school peppier, and engaging with people more intentionally.

Every week I would go, I would sit in the last seat in the last row. As I sat in the seat, I found myself gazing at the stage and hanging on every word being spoken instead of scanning the crowd looking for girls to meet like the first time. It was as if the speaker and I were the only ones in the whole world.

As time went on, I found out that previous messages from the gathering were accessible on a podcast. This was great news for me because I was so eager to hear more. I wasn't sure if I were sold on the whole church thing, but I couldn't stop consuming the information they were presenting. I downloaded the app and saw, not only were there a few weeks, every single week's message since the beginning of the gathering (which was about a year and half prior) was available. Needless to say, I was going to have enough to listen to for quite some time. I didn't hesitate to get started.

Going to the gathering also sparked my interests elsewhere in the church. It eventually led me to start volunteering. I found out they had a high school ministry. It seemed pretty interesting so I decided to sign up. (I'll go into more detail about my volunteering in a later chapter.)

As I went each and every week to the gathering and the high school ministry, I started feeling like I was missing something. Time and time again, I would hear about this relationship with God but still had no idea what it meant or looked like or how to have it. This was always one of my main frustrations growing up that was never explained to me.

As I continued to go, it seemed like everyone around me, especially the students, were so much farther ahead of me in their faith and their understanding of faith. I thought to myself, *I had to do something to change this.* No one likes to feel like the one who has no clue what's going on.

That night, which was around mid to late September, I went home and grabbed my laptop. In the search bar, I typed, "How do you have a relationship with God?"

I'm serious. I really searched those words. I didn't know how else to find out since people never fully answered the question when I would ask. It was always some vague answer that I couldn't quite grasp. Also I wasn't about to start asking people again because I was embarrassed I was going to the church and volunteering but didn't know about the main thing everyone talked about.

As I searched the question, ten or twelve steps with descriptions and pictures on "how to have a relationship with God" popped up. I read every word, scanned every picture with my searching eyes, and started to process for the first time some real and practical answers to what it looked like to have a relationship with God, at least so I thought.

One of the steps on the list was to pray. Check. I had been doing that for quite some time, even before the church. (More details on that to come). Another step was to read God's Word. I had to uncheck that one. I wasn't doing it because I didn't own a Bible. I had never owned Bible. So I got online and ordered a Bible to be overnight shipped to my apartment.

As I continued to read the list, I continued to determine whether I was doing or not doing the steps that came up in my search. The search was the only basis I had in terms of what a relationship could be at the time. It took a long time before I fully discovered it wasn't all about what I was doing but instead whom I was inviting into my life, which I still needed to discover more.

Here is an excerpt of a journal entry prayer where I later reflected on this understanding I came to grasp.

*11/12/16*

*Heavenly Father, There are so many times I feel I am reaching out for something and I work on my outside with expectations it will improve my inside. I feel often, if I do these outward things, it will improve my relationship with you and how you view me. I feel this is a practice from my past. Please help me to not reach out and improve my outside. Help me to make a home for you inside of me, a place that is calm, at peace, confident, kind, patient, understanding, humble, and, most important, all for you, centered on you, and willing to trust you. Amen.*

## The Answer

A few weeks had gone by since my search on a relationship with God. One of the things I was doing systematically since the night I searched online was reading the Bible. Aside from a brief period here and there in my life, I had never really read it before, let alone opened it. All of my knowledge about God, Jesus, and faith were from what people had taught me or told me to believe, and we know how much frustration and gaps that brought on.

One night, I was reading my Bible when a thought came into my head, *Why did Jesus have to die?* I had heard tons of explanations before that Jesus died for our sins and He died so we could have a relationship with God, but I never had heard it explained to me why He had to die in the first place. What was the original problem that led to it all?

Since my search on having a relationship with God was so successful, I figured I should search this new question that was bouncing around in my head. I pulled out my laptop, opened up the search engine, and typed in "Why did Jesus have to die?"

Article after article, site after site, started flooding my computer. I had no idea where to start. At first, I thought I would just read the first result that popped up and be done with it, but something held me up before committing to the plan. One thing I had learned in my readings of the Bible was that I had been taught a lot of information taken out of context. This was a warning flag for me. Being the self-proclaimed researcher I am, I decided, if I were going to discover the true meaning and answer of this question, I would need to read multiple sources, cross-reference them with each other, and ultimately check with what it said in the Bible.

Source after source I searched. With a Bible open on my lap while about ten windows were opened on my laptop, I searched. I started to discover what had taken place in the very beginning. It was saying God had created man and woman and left them to tend to the garden of Eden. They were allowed to eat anything in the garden except for fruit from a specific tree. If they were to eat from this tree, they would die. They were to die for going against God.

I continued to read how a serpent tempted them to eat the fruit. They ended up eating it, using the free will God had provided them, thinking God was withholding things from them. That moment was the first sign of sin in the world and the downfall of mankind. However, instead of being immediately put to death for their sin, they were banished from the garden, separated from God, and their eternal lives they were intended to have ended as God had promised. They would ultimately die.

As my searching led me deeper into this, I discovered, time and time again, sin continued to present itself as the flaws of people spread. God then made a covenant, an agreement, with

Noah, a man He found in great favor, that He would not lay waste to the earth ever again after the flood that had wiped out everyone except Noah's family and all the animals on the ark.

Following this covenant, God presented a series of rules and regulations to Moses and his people of ways to live clean lives and lead people out of their sinful ways and into the harmony and relationship God designed for humans. One of these rules was how the people were to pay for their sins. Something had to die as a result and payment for sin. To make this payment, a perfectly unblemished animal had to be sacrificed. This, however, was only a temporary payment. People continued to sin and fall short of the glory of God. Perfect harmony was not restored, and sacrifices continued on.

Through the years, God spoke through various prophets, announcing one day a new covenant would be established. This covenant would replace the old covenant and be the final piece for mankind to be in harmony and relationship with God. A final sacrifice to pay for all sins would one day be presented. This sacrifice was to be Jesus.

In knowing mankind could not fully pay for their sins and how all fell short of the glory of God, God took the form of a human being, born as a baby and growing up as a boy and young man named Jesus. Both fully human and fully divine, He was tempted with all the things anyone else would be tempted in life by, and He stayed perfect and sinless.

As the unblemished Lamb of the world, He sacrificed His perfect self to pay for all past, present, and future sins in the world. This was the final sacrifice needed for mankind to have the ability, if they chose, to be in perfect harmony and relationship with God.

I continued on to discover Jesus died. However, death did not defeat Him. Three days later, He rose from the dead and walked in flesh on this earth, spreading the good news that the eternal life that was once lost had now been resurrected as He ascended into heaven and left the world with the Holy Spirit to live inside of us and guide us through life.

Tears rolled down my face like a river dam had just broken. My hands outstretched to the ceiling of my bedroom as a smile was trying to form on my face. My shouting kept interrupting the smile. "Yes! Yes! Yes!" I shouted from my mouth in perfect unison with my hands clenching together and pushing upward as if I were trying to punch through the ceiling.

Finally, after so many years, I had my answer. I understood why Jesus had to die. Every sin I ever committed, was currently committing, and was to commit should have resulted in my immediate death and separation from God and eternal life forever. However, Jesus took the weight, the pain, and the punishment for each and every sin of mine before I was ever breathed into existence.

I had never felt a love like that before. My body was rushing with warm feelings as cold bumps covered my skin like scales. "Yes" was all I could say over and over again. This feeling couldn't be expressed in any other way, and even now as I am writing, words can't do it justice. All I could say was "Yes."

Here is the very first journal entry prayer I ever wrote that took place around this exact time I made this discovery. One can see through these words that I was slowly discovering more but still struggling with my past and needed some final clarity that was soon to come.

*10/11/16*

*Heavenly Father, I can't even express in words how truly grateful I am to have you in my life. I get in tears when I even try to understand how much my life and my outlook on life have changed since I have found you. I feel like this time I have found you for real. I'm starting to understand how you speak to us and what your message is to us. My biggest fear, Lord, is that I will not be able to sustain my love, worship, and complete focus on you.*

*I have a tendency to get super passionate and involved with something, but as time moves on, I lose interest as my life gets busy. This has happened in the past with my worship. I feel, however, I am older, more mature, and in the right environments to worship more truly. I love you, God, so much, and I am finally seeing how nothing in my life was created or accomplished by me. Instead, you did it all. Lord, please help my faith stay with me, and be the center of my entire life in a real way forever. Amen.*

## The Balcony

Now that I understood the reason behind Jesus's death and how to have a relationship with God, I walked with a kick in my step that a freight train couldn't stop. It was as if my eyes were opened to the world for the first time. Everything seemed brighter, everyone seemed more important, and beauty was seen with every blink. Life finally had purpose.

There was only one final thing left that I needed more clarity on and understanding behind. The first night, Clay said to lean on God and to trust Him with our lives. I had heard this time and time again on the nights since then. I didn't really understand what that looked like or why I would do it. The greatest thing was that someone was about to help me over this one final barrier.

As I walked out of the school for the day sometime in late October, I received a call from David, whom I met with a month or so back when I was starting to volunteer with the high school ministry. He worked for the church, and we had become somewhat of acquaintances. He invited me to come over and hang at his apartment if I were interested.

I couldn't say yes fast enough. At the time, even though I was attending the church, volunteering in the high school ministry, and personally having massive faith breakthroughs, I had yet to actually hang out with someone from the church. Needless to say, I was super excited.

Up a flight of stairs and a little way down an open corridor, I headed into David's apartment. He showed me around, and we made our way out onto his back balcony, where he had two lawn chairs set up. The sun was starting to set, and a beautiful view was in front of us as we looked over the rest of the apartment complex. Casual conversation took place for quite a while as the day turned to night.

Randomly, I got the idea to let David know I had finally completed all my paperwork to officially become a volunteer in the church's system. I had been doing various little volunteer jobs but hadn't officially become a volunteer just yet. He nodded and acknowledged what I had said but didn't seem to respond. There was this look on his face like he was straining to hold back what he truly wanted to say. As forward as I am, I insisted on him speaking what he wanted to say.

He stated that he had looked through my application, and while looking at it, he mentioned coming across where I had written about baptism. I could feel the blood draining from my hands as I clenched the side of the chair. This was the one part of my application that took the longest to complete, and I really was hoping I would never have to answer for it.

When I was completing the application, I arrived at the section for me to explain baptism and whether I had been baptized or not. This always had been a sore subject for me. I never really understood what baptism represented and why it was done. This was another one of those things that wasn't really ever fully explained. On top of that, I was nervous and afraid this would be the deciding factor of whether I could keep volunteering or not. Not sure of what to say, I looked up some very generic info on baptism, tied in a little of what I thought I knew, and typed it down.

"Tell me what baptism means to you," David asked.

I froze in fear. *Oh no*, I thought.

"Umm ... I think baptism is deciding to put your faith in Jesus Christ." Not entirely sure what that even meant, I was surprised those words came out of my mouth. My mind raced back to a few weeks prior when a few kids got baptized during the high school service and all of them were describing how they put their faith in Jesus. I guess that was where I got the idea.

"Do you understand why baptism represents putting your faith in Jesus?" David asked.

"Umm, to be honest, no, not really," I clambered.

"Baptism is a symbol of someone publicly professing that he or she has made a conscious decision to follow Jesus Christ. What this decision represents is the understanding that he or she has lived in sin, and no matter what the person does, the sin can't be fixed, gotten rid of, or paid for by the person. This sin has caused the person to be separated from God," he explained.

"Yea, yea, I remember reading about this," I said with a little more excitement in my voice as I interrupted him.

"That's great, man! Now God sent His Son Jesus to this earth as one who was both fully human and fully divine. His Son died for the debt of all our sins, resurrected from the dead, and ascended into heaven. Now through the resurrection, those who believe in Him will no longer be separated from God, can have a relationship with Him, and can have eternal life one day in heaven. Baptism also is a representation that one is going to turn away from a sinful life and turn toward a Jesus life. What do you think about that?" David asked.

"Hmmm, it all seems to make sense and go along with what I have been recently learning," I said very softly.

"Do you see how it is a little different from what you put down on your application?"

"Yea, does this mean I can't volunteer anymore?" I gasped.

"No, not at all. You are more than welcome to still serve," he said, smiling.

"Then what does it matter if I were baptized or not? I believe in Jesus and understand everything you have said. If it is just a symbol of something, why do it?" I asked, very confused and almost annoyed as you could hear the stress in every word I spoke.

Once again, a smile shone across David's face bigger than ever as he said, "I am glad you asked. Lots of people tend to be confused about the same thing. People don't understand the importance of publicly stating that they are choosing to follow Jesus. I want to show you a few things that might help clear up some of your confusion."

"Uhh … ok," I expelled.

He proceeded to show me what Jesus's last command was to His followers before ascending into heaven. "Jesus stated to go and make followers of Him by baptizing them and making sure they follow everything He has commanded. In doing this, Jesus promises to be with us always. By publicly sharing the inward decision one has made to follow Jesus, we are able to follow Jesus's last command."

"How?" I blurted out before David could start his next sentence.

"I'm glad you asked." His smile almost touched both his ears. "When you tell people about the life you had lived relying on yourself and how, no matter what you did, things weren't ever good enough and a lot of times resulted in failure, people are able to connect with you and your story. Then when you say that, because of the failure, you chose to turn your life over to Jesus and rely on Him instead of yourself, you shine a light on a solution, the solution they could also turn to.

"The best thing is, while sharing these things, you are sharing how much your life has changed because of Jesus. This opens people's eyes to the power of Jesus in our lives. This can result in them choosing to follow Him as well, just like Jesus's last command stated.

"Our main purpose on this earth is to glorify God with our lives and share the good news of Jesus to as many people as possible. Through baptism, we can live out that purpose in such a powerful way. You never know the lives you will affect by your public baptism." David finished up. (There is more on that impact in a later chapter.)

"Hmm … ok. I understand," I slowly muttered. "I mean, I guess my life has changed since I started going to the church. I am a lot happier than I was before, and I have felt really connected for the first time in a long time. However, I don't really understand the whole thing of following Jesus and turning my life over to Him. What do you mean?"

"Let me show you one more thing. There's this guy I have watched preach for years. He actually kind of reminds me of you and what I think you would be like if you preached. A sermon he preached a while back should connect to what we are talking about and what Christ does in our lives when we turn it over to Him."

David opened up his laptop and pulled up this video of a sermon titled "Just Call Me Jacob" by Steven Furtick. This sermon talked about how Jacob was one of two sons of Isaac. Being the younger son, Jacob did not have the birthright when his father Isaac would die. The birthright was basically an inheritance of the majority of the father's possessions. Jacob did not like that he would not receive the inheritance, so he devised a plan to trick his older brother, Esau.

Esau was a hunter while Jacob was more accustomed to being around the home, cooking and such. One day, when Esau came in from a hunt, Jacob was cooking a stew. Esau was so hungry and worn out from the hunt that he indicated he would die if he didn't get something to eat.

He begged Jacob for some of the stew. Instead of Jacob just

giving over the stew, he said he would only do it if Esau gave him his birthright. Believe it or not, Esau did exactly that. Esau gave away his birthright as the firstborn to the inheritance. Jacob's trick had worked. However, this was not the only time Jacob would trick Esau.

Furtick continued in the sermon, explaining how there were two very important things during the time period: the birthright and the blessing. The blessing was the most important thing to receive. Before one's father died, he would bless the son, explaining his inheritance as well as his approval of the son going forward, thereby casting vision for the future in the presence of the Lord. This blessing was also to go to Esau. However, there was a plan in place for Jacob to receive this as well.

Isaac's wife, Rebekah, heard Isaac telling Esau to go out and hunt, come back, and prepare a meal for them. Then he would receive the blessing. Rebekah told Jacob to do the sneaky thing and to disguise himself as Esau so he could receive the blessing instead. Jacob did exactly this and stole Esau's blessing from him.

As the sermon continued, Furtick discussed an account that took place later on in Jacob's life where he was wrestling with a man. This man he was wrestling with turned out to be God. After they were done wrestling, Jacob said he would not let the man go unless He blessed Jacob right there. The man asked Jacob for his name, and Jacob said his name was Jacob. Following this, the man said this would no longer be Jacob's name. He now would be called Israel.

At this point in the sermon, I was getting a little worn out. I had just heard three different accounts of this man Jacob's life, and I was still trying to figure out what all of this had to do with what David was explaining about following Jesus and turning my life over to Him. I'm sure you are feeling this right now too. However, I continued to listen.

Furtick finished up the sermon by describing the identity crisis that Jacob had. Jacob was not supposed to be the firstborn with the birthright or receive his father's blessing. However, he tricked Esau and took on his identity to receive these things. The whole time Jacob was trying to be someone else. He was not being true to who he was as Jacob but was fighting after being Esau.

I sat a little closer as it continued. This identity crisis led to the moment where he was wrestling with God. Jacob demanded to be blessed, and God asked him his name. Jacob could have lied like he had for most of his life. However, at that very moment, Jacob humbled himself, and in the face of God, he admitted who he really was. He was Jacob.

God could rid Jacob of the false identity he once lived by once he finally took on his true identity. God could now give him a whole new one. Jacob didn't just receive a new name but also a blessing of the life he was going to live from that point on. His new name was a symbol of him leaving his old ways behind and stepping into the new ways of God.

"So what did you think?" David asked.

A long pause filled the balcony air as I pondered over what was being pieced together in my mind. I looked down at my feet.

"Ummm," I started to mutter as if I forgot how to speak. "I am Jacob."

"Tell me more about what you mean," David said calmly.

"I am Jacob. My whole life, I have tried to take on the identity of literally everything and everyone else instead of becoming who I truly am and was meant to be. You've heard my story. All the things I was into were all me trying to become something I was never meant to be."

"Who are you meant to be, Philip?" David asked with his voice getting so soft that the wind almost masked its very existence.

"I am meant to fully be a follower of Jesus," I said as if the sentence started as a question and finished as an exclamation. "I finally realize, until I reveal who I really am, all the things I have tried to be, and all the failures that have resulted from me living for myself, like Jacob did, God can never reveal to me who I am meant to become and give me a new name, a new life."

"And what name would the name be?" David asked.

"Child of God." My eyes were moving back and forth in rapid pace as I tried to ponder the feeling that was coming over me as I said the last statement. "David, I want to fully put my faith in Christ and trust Him with everything. I am done trying to live life by my own ways. I want to follow the ways He has set out for me."

Here is an excerpt of a journal entry I wrote later on where I looked back on my identity struggle and what I began to realize.

4/11/17

*Going back to July, I was living a mess of a life through an even bigger mess of an identity. Then I found Jesus. Everything changed. I stopped trying to find my identity in myself or create a false identity and instead started to find my true identity in Christ Jesus. This is still so far away from being complete, and I don't know if it will ever be. The important thing is that I'm searching and not stopping. I have learned so much in these past months about the real me and what caused the fake me. I find myself dying to the old, familiar identity that has suffocated me and my truest potential for so long. This is the battle I fight. This battle already has and will continue to expose flawed, vulnerable, or just plain fake parts about myself, but I must continue on to find my true identity in Christ. I need to stop trying to fit in or stand out and just be firm and still in whom I am in Christ. I have a long, tough battle ahead of me in this, and it is important to not get weary when I fall or struggle. I must continue to find my true self in Him because it is only in that true self that He can work and really make flourish.*

I continued telling David that I wanted to scream out to the world that I am a child of God, and then I said the magical phrase to him, "David, I want to get baptized."

To write the words David smiled wouldn't even do the moment justice as to the feeling that filled the balcony at that very instant on that very night. As if it were completely orchestrated by God through David, the gospel was presented to me.

I had the final truths I needed as to the reason to follow Jesus. No longer was I to question whether I was into the whole church thing or not. The local church had officially taken hold. I walked away that night and drove home a changed man forever.

Here is an excerpt from a journal entry prayer I wrote shortly after this moment took place.

*10/24/16*

*Heavenly Father, For some time now, I have wanted to find my own way. I feel now I am able to properly accept you publicly as my Lord and Savior. Amen.*

## December 18, 2016

I walked through the familiar room where the gathering took place every Sunday night. However, tonight, it was as if it took on a new look. It was an unfamiliar one to my eyes. The chairs were arranged in a horseshoe shape around a small center stage that was in the middle. Just to the left of the stage was this black, rectangular object on wheels that had stairs leading up the side of it. Water filled it. Right in front of the black rectangle were about fifty chairs that all had a "reserved" sign on them.

I stood in front of those chairs, pondering over where I was just a few months prior—empty, alone, scared, and just about ready to call it quits on the whole thing called life. Now I was staring at fifty chairs that were soon to be filled with fifty people who had impacted my life throughout the years and over the past few months. Not to mention the couple hundred other seats that made up the rest of the horseshoe of regular attendees.

Right in the front of these chairs would soon be a friend named Leigh Ann whom I met in seventh grade. She tried so hard to bring me to Christ and church but was always met with my fighting resistance. This night was just a few days before her family was moving away from Georgia. She was to sit there with her two baby boys.

Not too far away from her seat was going to be where my friends, Micah and Ashley, were to sit. Ashley and I had been best friends all throughout college. We used to run the bars together. She then met Jesus and became a fully devoted follower of Him, leaving me to the bars by myself as I sunk into wallowing depression. She was going to be sitting next to her fiancé, Micah.

Together, during my final years of college, where my drinking and outlook on life got to be the worst, they tried harder than ever to introduce me to Jesus. They constantly tried to bring me to church, but they always came up short. I would bash them, yell at them, and make fun of them. They never lost hope, however.

Right behind them were the seats where some fraternity brothers and their wives were to sit. Chief among this group were Matt and Kayla, who walked alongside me patiently and slowly as I began to discover who Jesus was. Also sitting in the section of chairs was my partner in crime, James, whom I mentioned in the prologue as the inspiration for the title of this book.

Just toward the back of the fifty reserved chairs was going to be several teachers from the school where I taught. They got to witness firsthand on a daily basis the transformation my life had made as I began walking in faith and going to church. Among them was the one person I had all of this to thank, the person who had no idea how God was going to use her to forever change an almost complete stranger's life with a little conversation we were going to have. Right there was where Heather was going to be sitting, as her infectious smile was to fill the room.

As I took one last glance out at the empty chairs before the doors were to open, I pictured all the faces that were going to fill the room of all the people I had met at the church leading up to this point. I thought about all the people who were going to be in the seats, the ones who helped me gain the understandings of Christ's love and community through our multiple dinners that we had after the Sunday night gatherings. All these people had helped remind me that God would never allow me to be alone.

There were a few people who weren't going to be sitting in the seats, however. Due to various circumstances, my family was not able to be in attendance. (They later would watch the recording online.) One other person who was not going to be sitting in the seats was David.

You might be thinking, *How could the man God used to present the gospel to you and explain baptism to you not be in the seats, watching you make this public profession of your faith?*

Well, as I turned around to face the portable baptistery, the black, rectangular object on wheels, I saw David standing by it, going over the instructions with the baptism coordinator, Beth. He smiled over at me as he prepared to be the very person whom God not only chose to present the gospel to me but the guy God chose to baptize me.

The service started with Clay welcoming everybody to the gathering and explaining how tonight was going to be a special night because tonight the gathering was going to be celebrating a baptism and only the second baptism that had taken place there before. He stated how I was going to be getting baptized, and then he cued it to the screens to have everyone watch my testimony video. Below is the dialogue from the video.

"My name is Philip Floor. Growing up, I always felt so distant from God. I had friends along the way, like Leigh Ann and Ashley, who tried to show me the way to God, but I was always living for myself and was slipping away.

"After college, it all came crumbling down. I started to develop severe anxiety and depression and was battling with physical illness. I was in and out of doctors' offices, and after one of my visits, I was told I needed to go to the Atlanta Cancer Center to get further testing.

"After two horrible weeks, I found out that there was nothing wrong. So I asked myself, *Why do I feel so sick?* So I went to my mother for advice, and she asked me a very simple question, 'When was the last time you talked to God?' At that point, I realized that I felt this way because I didn't have God in my life. So from that point forward, I started talking to God. Things got better but not great.

"Then my friend Heather suggested that I go to this Sunday night gathering. I went that night, and the topic was 'Lonely But Not Alone.' After listening to that message and hearing the lyrics to 'When the Fight Calls,' I realized that I had no control over my life and I needed a Savior. I don't need to carry the weight of my sin because Jesus already did that for me. He gave up His life for me and chose to pay for my sins so I could have a relationship with God. I know now that I can trust Him with my life and that He promises to never leave me.

"From there I went back and listened to every podcast from the Sunday night gathering since the very beginning. I signed up to volunteer with the high school ministry and the elementary ministry. I signed up to join some events for singles, started meeting with a small group, and just recently sought out a mentor through the church.

"The happiness, the joy, and the relationships that I have made in the past five months are more than in the previous twenty-four years. I'd love to thank Leigh Ann, Ashley, Kayla, David, everyone at the gathering, my friend Heather, and, most importantly, my mother. Tonight I want to publicly profess that Jesus Christ is my Lord and Savior."

The video ended, and the people in attendance started to cheer.

"Yea, c'mon. Give it up for Phil," David began to say. "Philip,

I know we've had multiple conversations about this from sitting on my back porch or from me driving in the car and you calling me to talk about this very moment. Just to know your past and know that you were walking through life carrying its burdens, its worries, its anxieties, and its struggles on your own and you were being crushed.

"Then you realized 'I want to give this to God' and 'I don't have to do life alone, and God can carry these burdens, struggles, and anxieties for me.' I want you to know that that's not just a truth about your past. That's a truth also about your future. For the rest of your life, you don't have to be crushed by life because Jesus was crushed for you. Then He rose in a glorious resurrection, and you get to experience life to the fullest.

"So I want you to go from here tonight knowing you can always hand God your worries and anxieties. Based on your profession of Jesus going to the cross for you and rising again, it's my privilege in front of your friends, people who love you, and people you love to baptize you in the name of the Father, Son, and Holy Spirit."

The people cheered as I was lowered down into the water and then was lifted out. I wiped my face off, pointed up to the heavens, and then hugged David with the biggest hug ever as all those friends I mentioned before wiped away the tears in their eyes.

On December 18, 2016, after years of waiting for this moment and all the people trying to lead me to it, I was finally baptized, pronouncing that Jesus Christ is my Lord and Savior.


**Words for Thought**

*Reasons People Have Left*

Many people's experiences with the local church and faith in general have common themes attached to them. One of the most common themes is how things were never fully explained. We are often taught the "what to believe" but not the "why to believe."

People would explain how there is a God and a Jesus and we should go to church and believe in them. However, if you would ask questions about why to do all of those things, the usual response was "because that's what you do." Following the response, the person usually tried to avoid the rest of the conversation.

If you are anything like me, you have probably experienced similar things in the church and in faith. Eventually, because of this, when times got tough, answers weren't given, and fake people attending church were discovered, we decided to turn away from the church, planning to never turn back. My pastor often explains this as "our childhood faith not being able to hold up against our adult problems and questions."

There are so many people who have left the church, like myself, usually not for any reason having to do with God, but usually having to do with how God was presented to them. Confusion, misconceptions, false teachings, and forced beliefs eventually drove us away from the church for good.

The main reason why I was so bitter to church in general was because I always wanted answers to questions that people avoided. It made me so mad how anyone would just mindlessly go to a building, sing some songs, hear a message, and believe in something "because that's what you do."

Fortunately, after my first night returning to the church, all of the things I wanted answers to my whole life started being brought up. This broke down the wall I fought so hard to keep up about the local church and solidified faith in me for good. My hope is, through these stories, some of the things that have held you up or turned you away from the church could finally be put to rest so you can discover the joy that awaits you. I understand though that more explanation might need to be provided, especially around the relationship we can have with God.

*Relationships*

The relationships one has in his or her life can oftentimes determine the quality of that life. If a person is not actively engaged with at least one other, life seems to start to not have much meaning to it. However, things get a whole lot brighter and have more of a purpose the second someone else comes into the picture and a relationship starts to form.

Now this relationship I am talking about isn't limited to just a dating or marriage context. These relationships can be between friends, family, colleagues, and so on. When two people are actively engaged in walking through life together, a relationship has the potential to form.

Many times in these relationships that we form, we miss the mark on what is of the most importance. We think presenting gifts, doing helpful deeds, and spending brief periods of time together are what it takes to keep the relationship alive and growing. None of these things are bad or wrong. Oftentimes though, we find out that, underneath the outer coating of the relationship, a completely hollow inside is present.

When things go wrong in life, promises aren't kept, and hurtful things are said, the outer shell breaks, and the relationship falls apart. Due to the emptiness that has billowed underneath the shell, the relationship never had a chance of standing its ground.

This is very commonly found among those in the church environment and was sure found for me over so many years. Doing all the outside steps of reading the Bible, going to church, listening to Christian music, treating people nicely, donating money, and so forth all make many feel as if they are sustaining and growing the relationship they have with God. Don't get me wrong. All of those things are wonderful. They just aren't of the most importance.

Those things oftentimes solidify the outer shell of an appearance that the person is "holy," but not much is taken into account of what is happening underneath the shell. When times get tough, obstacles are put in the way, and things don't pan out the way they were supposed to, many of those same people turn their backs on faith, God, and the church. The outer shell cracks, and the hollowness inside doesn't stand the chance against life.

In any given relationship, the thing of most importance is how much we let the other person involved in the relationship into our lives, hearts, and struggles. Whether it is a mom, a friend, a husband, or whoever, the relationship can only truly be defined by how much we are letting the person past our outer, protective shell and into who we really are and what we are really going through.

When we let those people in, they are able to walk alongside us when times get tough, motivate us when we need it the most, and be there for us when everyone else has turned his or her back. Letting the person into your life in this way is what separates him or her from the billions of other people who pass by on this planet. All the other stuff is great, but the privilege of the relationship is the things the special one knows about you that others don't. I'll say this again. The privilege of the relationship is the things the special one knows about you that others don't.

If you have relationships you are actively engaged with in your life, consider this. Right now and going forward, consider what those people are allowed access to that the rest of the world isn't. All the other stuff is great, but until they are allowed past the outer, perfect shell as well as the things that everyone else knows, there is no promise for a true relationship to form.

This was a realization I had to come to through my life with many people but most of all with God. I tried so many times to build this relationship with Him by doing all the things I mentioned early. However, as soon as things weren't glorious, I packed up and ran. Eventually though, I discovered that, in the end, none of those things really mattered if I weren't going to give God the privilege that others didn't have. Until I was going to invite Him in past my outer shell, into my heart, and reveal all of my struggles, there was never really going to be a relationship. Before I could do this though, I needed to discover why.

### Discovering the Why

Whether you are in school, at a job, or around your house, lots of things need to get done. Doing the laundry, completing the expense report, and writing the paper are all tasks that are very essential to each of their environments. However, they can be some of the hardest things to find motivation for. Many times, these are the things that make their way to the bottom of the to-do lists that reoccur day after day until you are either out of clothes, about to be fired, or going to fail the class.

Ok, maybe that's a little extreme, but they are things that do often get put off. For me, the most common thing I put off is taking out the trash. I don't know why it is, but I just hate taking out the trash. Always thinking there is just enough room on top to make the perfect "Trash Mountain," as I like to call it, I steer clear as long as I can to taking it out. My roommates at the time, if you are reading this now, completely know what I am talking about. Sorry, fellas!

With all these things that are essential in our lives but so commonly ignored or put aside, one major thing is often absence. That thing is the "why" behind doing the task. Yes, anyone can say why something should be done, but saying it and embracing it are two very different things.

When we are simply saying why something should be done, we are merely providing a specific set of words in the right order to justify an action. There often is no depth to the statement. It is usually presented as a hollow reason to a task, calling on us to complete. This can be seen oftentimes when we are young and we ask our parents why we have to go to bed at a certain time. The response is usually something like "because I say so" or "so you can get a good night's sleep."

These statements often left us resenting the task even more than before. Those reasons never really sunk in with us. They were never things we could cling to as inspiration to complete the task. The same thing applies in any aspect of life where something or someone is calling on you to do something.

Hanging out with certain people, doing specific things, or believing in particular beliefs are all things called on us throughout life. Whether these things are presented to us by others, the media, or just the general order of life's events, if we don't discover the "why" behind them, the real "why," the one that we can actually embrace, they will usually get put off or become unsustainable.

When we really discover the "why" behind something and it becomes something we embrace, this is when real power can take over and sustainable joy can set in. This had to happen to me in order to officially commit to accepting the local church as a place I would no longer pass up on. You might be in the same boat.

If you have considered giving faith a try or going back to church or realized that you can't seem to keep up a consistent attendance there, do the searching that many people don't do. Ask yourself why should you go. When you discover the answer to this particular question that you can fully get behind, you will be surprised what can happen, how much less frequently you miss church, and how much easier it is to walk back in.

*Identity*

"Who am I?" This is a question many people seem to ponder as they go through life. Discovering one's identity has proven to be a challenge. With the media and social media portraying a picture of the people we should desire to become, it can be hard to really embrace whom we were designed to be.

This struggle can lead people into difficult situations during their pursuit. Going down paths of drugs, promiscuous sexual behavior, crime, depression, anxiety, and so forth can often be results of people trying to discover who they are. Going along with others and desperate attempts to fit in plague the minds and hearts of so many leading us to do things we normally wouldn't consider doing and providing us with false identities we were never meant to have.

I am going to make a bold statement and say I was one of the guiltiest people of all in falling trap to these false identities. Through various bad decisions and attempts to be anyone and everyone aside from my true self, I was lost. Not knowing who Philip was but only knowing who everyone else thought he was and wanted him to be led me to making most of these bad decisions.

Maybe you have been in this situation before or are currently in this circumstance. You find yourself doing things without much understanding as to why you are doing them. Possibly you like things or people because that is what you think those around you want from you. It could even be that you are trapped in a lifestyle you never could have imagined for yourself that has brought on deep shame.

If this is you, then you are like how I was through most of the stories in this chapter. I had no idea why I did the things I did, liked the things I liked, and believed the things I believed. All I could eventually credit it to be was my search for an identity. Unfortunately I kept providing myself with a false identity instead.

Through discovering whom Jesus says I am, I was able to find a way out of the trapped lifestyle I was living in. Realizing that I didn't have to be what I thought others wanted me to be was one of the most freeing things I embraced. God says who I am and who all of you are, and by embracing and becoming that, the searching for identity comes to an end. Eventually you are just sitting in the comfort, glory, and freedom that God provides.

Maybe you aren't there yet. That is ok if you aren't. If the whole God thing hasn't settled into your thoughts, there still is one thing I want to leave you with in regards to identity. As you continue to search and discover who you are, consider this: are the people and things you are surrounding yourself with wanting stuff for you or from you? When surrounded by all the things and people that want stuff from you, false identities sink in. You are usually being used to please others.

However, when surrounded by things and those who want stuff for you, true identities sink in. You are surrounding yourself with people and things that want to truly better who you are. They actually care about your well-being and whether you are in a healthy place or not.

*Challenge*

Regardless of where you are at in your journey, I hope there were some things in this chapter that you can apply to the areas that have the greatest needs. Consider the reasons that have led you to walk away from the church or not give faith a try. You might just be surprised that there is a possibility that what is holding you up has nothing to do with who Jesus is. If you are already in church, think about ways you can better help lead and disciple those who are walking out the church doors every week, never to return.

Assess the relationships that you have. Look where you can better allow those special few into your lives and your hearts. The freedom and comfort experienced by sharing your struggles with others might surprise you. Ultimately I hope you will do this with Jesus. Consider allowing Him into your heart and telling Him your struggles. I challenge you to give Jesus a try for the next thirty days. It may be the thirty days that change the course of your life forever. What harm could come from giving Jesus a chance?

This, however, can't be fully possible without discovering the "why." When you discover why you do what it is you do in life or what others want you to do, a motivation and strength shows up like none other. Whether it is faith or something like eating healthier, discover why you should or want to do it. Having a cheering section is great, but if you don't have one inside yourself, the thing you are doing will be almost impossible to sustain. Discovering that "why" will generate the cheering section in you.

Finally, I hope you consider those who want things for you and turn away from those who want things from you. In your pursuit to discover who you are, always remember, whether you believe it or not, you are a child of God and He wants to reveal who He created you to be.

# CHAPTER 3
# Chasing Control

*As I stated in the letter to my readers, some of these stories start before others and end around the same time. This chapter is one of those stories. This chapter takes place two years before all the previous events that have been shared so far in this book. However, the ending happened after the events took place. As you read this chapter, hopefully, a lot of context to things previously shared and the backstory will come to light.*

It was over. My first year of teaching had come to the end, and I was heading into the summer of 2015. This summer was to be like no other due to the circumstances surrounding it. Every summer prior, I was looking toward something. Each year, my eyes were glued on what was ahead. If I just finished third grade, I was looking toward fourth grade, seventh grade toward eighth grade, senior year to entering college, and finishing college toward my first year in a job. There was always something on the horizon.

However, this summer was different. I wasn't looking toward anything; nothing new was up ahead. The only thing in sight was a repeat of the previous year teaching at the same place, the same grade, the same age, and the same subjects. Never before had I found myself in that position.

Yes, it was exciting in a way that I would get to spend another year learning to grow in my craft, but there wasn't the same newness all the other years brought. Due to the absence of newness, I found myself pondering "What's next?" for the first time in my life.

It was as if I had spent my entire existence living next to a huge mountain and everyone told me that one day I would reach the top. Each and every year, I made it a little farther up the mountain, but the top still didn't ever come into focus.

Then one day, I took those final steps. Three, two, one. I was there at the top, looking out and seeing what every person before me had described. The beauty and glory of reaching it was setting in. Then I found myself looking out and going "What's next?" My entire life was all about getting up to the top and never really thinking of much past that.

With that realization, I found myself in a slump going into the summer. To me, nothing was really up ahead. Without much hope, I started to enclose myself into my house. The days seemed to pass by as I stared on, watching TV show after TV show. It was completely beautiful outside; however, I sat in a bunker I had built for myself. It was almost as if it were a voluntary prison and I was there for an extended stay.

My outlook on life started to diminish as my feeling of worthlessness started to take hold. Along with that outlook, my health started to go right out the window. I was putting on weight faster than I could realize, and an overall feeling of sickness was becoming the new norm for me.

One night as I was going to bed, I looked at myself in the mirror and almost didn't recognize the man who was looking back: scraggly beard, large gut, and the same clothes I had been wearing for days. I was looking at a complete stranger. I couldn't believe what sitting around in sorrow had done to me.

Realizing a change needed to take place or the mirror was to be thrown out, I decided that the next day I would do one thing and one thing only: I would go to the gym. If nothing else were accomplished the next day, that was ok, just as long as I went to the gym. It didn't really matter what I did at the gym as long as I went.

Torment started to take over my mind as all the negative thoughts swarmed:

- "You are too out of shape!"
- "What is the point of going to the gym?"
- "You aren't an athlete anymore."
- "There is no hope for your future."
- "You still have to finish season four of the show you are watching."
- "What gym would you go to?"
- "What would you even do once you got there?"

Those last two questions actually reminded me of something. About a year before, I signed up for a gym and a personal trainer but never went. My brother calls this donating to a gym. Because of the fact that I never went and I couldn't cancel the services due to contractual obligations, the sessions just racked up on my account. Knowing this, I decided I would go to that gym and use up all of the personal training sessions I had—taking all the thirty-minute sessions, combining them into one-hour sessions, and going three days a week.

The next day, I got up, left the house, and started using the personal training services. I could write an entire comedy series on what those first few sessions were like due to how out of shape I was and how impersonal the "personal" trainer was. However, I'll hold my tongue. What draws me to this point in the story is what happened on one specific day at the gym that was set to start a change in my life forever.

I walked outside of my house in Roswell, Georgia, where I was living at the time, and drove to the gym for my personal training session at 8:00 a.m., as I had been doing for the past week or so. I was barely able to focus on the road ahead of me after not sleeping well the night before. I tried to force down my microwave oatmeal so I could consume some form of sustenance in my body before I got to the torture chamber that was my training session.

Walking in, I stretched on my own, and the session started. One exercise after another, my heart rate sped up faster and faster. Race cars barely top the speed my heart rate seemed to be going. I ran on the treadmill, did some medicine ball exercises, and then did the one thing that should be illegal, the ropes that you throw up and down to work your arms.

"You doing all right, Philip?" my trainer asked.

"Umm ... yea I'm ok, I guess. Didn't sleep much, but it's whatever," I stated.

"Ok, just let me know. You know the session before yours? The girl puked," the trainer shared with almost a proud smile crossing over her face.

*Puke? Great!* I thought to myself.

"Let's go ahead and do this push-up exercise," the trainer told me as she demonstrated it.

One rep after another, I went on through this exercise that I swear could be used as a punishment device for people. After the first set, I asked for the first time if I could get some water. Walking over to the fountain, I thought I was going to be the next one to puke. Brushing it off, I went on to complete the next set.

Standing up after the set, I rocked side to side and stated that I didn't feel so good. The trainer suggested I go sit down and eat a little something. Feeling super light-headed, I wobbled over to a chair as if I were about to pass out. Super nauseous, I tried as hard as I could to stop the feeling I was having, but it seemed to grow worse. This caused a deep panic inside me.

My trainer went over to the grocery store that was next to the gym and bought some Nutri-Grain bars and a Gatorade for me to eat and drink. I could barely force it down. About an hour later, I finally started to feel better. I stood up out of my chair very weak and confused and walked out of the gym as my trainer gave me the final bit of "training" for the day.

"Go get some rest," she stated.

Driving home all seemed like a blur. I walked into my house and my room, crawled into bed, and slept for most of the rest of the day. I woke up once or twice to go to the bathroom and eat a few crackers and then went back to sleep. I was done.

The next day I woke up and realized I didn't have any food in my house. So I decided to go to the grocery store. Getting ready and getting into my car, I started reflecting on what had happened the day before. It felt like it was a dream. I still couldn't really decide if it actually happened or not. All I knew was that I really didn't feel like myself. That panicked feeling was still very present inside of me.

On my way to the grocery store, which was only a few miles away, I continued to think about yesterday's events. All of a sudden, it happened for the first time. My mind seemed to go blank, my vision seemed to erase, and I realized I had driven past the store. The problem was, just a second before, I remembered still being about two miles away.

*What just happened?* I thought to myself. *Did I just black out? Is anyone hurt? Am I hurt? What is going on?* All these thoughts raced through my head. I couldn't figure out what had happened. All I could piece together was what had taken place yesterday and how it must be related. The fact was, I was two miles away from the store and in a matter of seconds I was passing the store. I instantly knew something was wrong.

I turned around to head home more confused than I had ever been in my life. I then called my mom to explain the events. She didn't seem super concerned as I had always been on more of the dramatic side of things when it came to medical stuff. She stated though that I should go to the doctor if I really felt like something was wrong. This is exactly what I did. I called my doctor and made an appointment for the next day.

As the rest of the day carried out, I consumed it with doing the one thing I could do best, research. I started searching the symptoms I had the day before and was continuing to have, trying to get a grasp on what could have caused this and attempting to figure out how worried I should be. This was my attempt at trying to control the situation.

The night was horrible. I couldn't sleep as my mind was flooded with concern and possible causes. I was nauseous, light-headed, and dizzy. You try searching those symptoms and see the horrors that can show up. And oh, did they show up more than ever. My symptoms could result from just being hungry to straight dying. I expected the worst, and so began the treacherous journey ahead.

## Rock Bottom

One doctor's visit after another came over the next two weeks, as my symptoms seemed to be getting worse. Frustration grew inside of me as a result of the doctors continuously saying they couldn't find anything that was causing all of the symptoms I was describing. I was very nauseous, losing weight fairly quickly, dizzy constantly, and starting to have freak-outs that I used to have in past years of my life. These were all very real symptoms that they could see, but no cause was being discovered.

I didn't have a diagnosis, so I decided I would take matters into my own hands. I continued to research my symptoms as more were starting to appear. I was determined to put a label on what was happening to me, thinking that would make things better.

I couldn't eat or sleep, I had a very erratic heart rate, and I was down a significant amount of weight in just a few weeks. I was feeling very weak. I realized these freak-outs that were happening could be the result of panic attacks, based on my research. Without an official diagnosis though, I wasn't convinced just yet. Whatever they were, they were making it very hard for me to be out in public places.

At first I couldn't go out to restaurants. Then it was stores. Shortly following that, I couldn't be in the car much. This eventually led to me not being able to go outside, period. The more and more symptoms I had, the more and more panicked I became. I continued to search for a solution, a diagnosis, something that would bring some piece to my mind. Every little odd feeling that would come across my body or thought in my head would spiral into one of those freak-outs and the feeling I was dying.

*I must be dying*, I thought to myself since no one could figure out what was wrong.

The doctors could clearly see what was happening to my body, however. I looked horrible. I was very pale, shaky, overly cautious, and protective. I looked like a very sick patient in a hospital.

It was now almost a month since the first moment at the gym. I tried everything to regain control over my health, my body, and my life with no luck. I couldn't figure out how one day at the gym could have spiraled all of this out of control. I decided I was going to continue to control the situation that led me to prescribe myself with a possible solution. I thought it might be some unhealthy habits I had developed that finally went haywire, so I started breaking them.

I had used tobacco regularly since I was a teenager. I quit it instantly. I was a heavy drinker. I quit. I also drank a lot of soda. I'm talking about a twelve-pack a day. I quit. I actually quit all caffeine at that point. I eliminated anything that I thought could have been contributing to my symptoms. You can imagine what your body does when you quit tobacco, alcohol, and caffeine all at the same time, cold turkey.

It was official. I had reached it, rock bottom. I had grown so weak that I could barely get off the couch. To add to it, I was having ten or so freak-outs a day. Still with no clue as to what was causing all of this, I knew my life was completely out of control and I had no control.

## It's Over

I woke up one morning and basically crawled downstairs. At that point, summer was halfway over, and I had been staying at my parents' house for a few weeks. I had grown so sick that I couldn't really take care of myself anymore. Life was at an all-time low, and it couldn't get much worse. Then my phone rang.

It was my doctor stating that some of my blood work results had come back and apparently I had a severely low platelet count in my blood. I instantly froze at attention.

*Could this be it? Could this be what had been causing all the problems since the day at the gym?* I thought to myself.

My doctor continued to say that she was referring me to this other doctor to get my blood further tested. She gave me the doctor's name, told me that my appointment was in two weeks, and said for me to have a good day.

*Have a good day?* I thought to myself. *What kind of garbage is that?*

As soon as the call ended, I opened up my search browser, as had become my normal routine, and I searched the name of the new doctor. The search result came back with something I wish I never saw. It turned out that the new doctor worked at the Atlanta Cancer Center. Yea, you read that right, the Cancer Center.

I instantly felt the first freak-out of the day coming on. I immediately opened up another search tab and searched "low platelet count" to find out exactly what all of that could mean. Out of all the results that showed up, one word stood out over the rest of possibilities, leukemia.

"Leukemia! Leukemia! I can't have that!" I screamed out, not realizing my dad had entered the room.

"What did you say?" my dad asked.

"My doctor just told me that I have a severely low platelet count and I need to go to the Atlanta Cancer Center for further testing. It looks like it could mean I have leukemia!" I said as fast as words could come out of someone's mouth.

"I'm sure it's nothing. Just a follow-up check to make sure they cover all their bases," my dad shared with the most laid-back tone ever.

Truly he could have said anything. I wasn't able to process anything except the word *leukemia*. I fell back down on the couch after realizing I had shot up when talking with my dad. I felt lower than I had ever felt before. Then I began the conversation with myself that is even hard to this day to believe I had as I am writing this chapter on a beach in Jacksonville.

"You are weak beyond anything you have ever experienced before," I stated to myself. "You can't even leave the house. You can't even fight the battles of your freak-outs. You don't even know what they are. How are you possibly going to fight a cancer battle? You can't! You're not strong enough! You will fail! Just ... end it ... now ..."

As those final words left my tongue, I lifted my head up from the lowered position it was in and just stared blankly in front as if I were peering into the darkest of darkness. Never in my life had that thought or option ever seemed so real.

Everything was pointing in my mind to the fact that, if I had cancer, I couldn't beat it. I at least couldn't beat it in the state I was in. So I figured I would save myself the trouble and end it.

Fortunately for me, I made a deal with myself. If the appointment I were to have in two weeks came back with a diagnosis of leukemia, I would end it. Until then, I would hold on.

## The One Thing

The day came as my mom and I entered the cancer center. Due to my freak-outs, I wasn't driving much at that point. I walked in to find out my fate. No one knew this was the fate I had decided, but to me, there really wasn't any other option. I had tried everything, and I only seemed to get worse. Living back at home, unable to take care of myself, I saw that there was no way I was going to be able to return to my job in the coming weeks. How could I take care of kids if I couldn't take care of myself?

I was in sheer panic while sitting and waiting for my results to come back. As soon as I sat down to wait, my body went into what seemed to be uncontrollable convulsions. This was a new symptom. Great! My body wouldn't stop shaking, and no matter how hard I tried to control it, the convulsions got worse and worse. I sat there for what seemed like hours. Then the news came.

"You're all good to go," the doctor said with confidence in his voice.

"Huh?" I questioned.

"It turns out that the vial they used to test your blood the first time had a recall on it because it makes platelets clump together, seeming as though you have a low platelet count," explained the doctor.

One would think I jumped up out of my seat and marched around the room in a celebration of life, but unfortunately, this was not the reaction I had. Confusion—and even some disgust— was sweeping through my mind as the storm inside of me was raining havoc. I couldn't believe it. This whole time, all this panic and everything my body was going through, all was pointing to a completely normal bill of health.

*How could this be?* I thought as I grabbed my things and made my way out to the car with my mom.

Leaning my head against the window as we drove back to my parents' house, I reflected on the past six weeks I had lived.

I examined the dark pits I had allowed my mind to go and the pincushion my body had become from all the medical tests, all for nothing.

Something was different this time coming back from the doctors. All the other visits left me frustrated that there still wasn't a diagnosis. This time, it was as if my mind had just woken up from a long sleep. The thought rang through my head that, if nothing had been uncovered through everything I went through, maybe there wasn't anything wrong to begin with.

By this point, I had moved back in with my parents, lost more pounds than I could remember, had my blood drawn four times, been to the doctor six times, had an ultrasound on my organs, and went to the cancer center for a slew of tests. Six weeks I had wasted of my life chasing something that was possibly never there.

From a reader's perspective, it might seem so simple and clear that nothing was ever wrong. However, when you were as far down the rabbit hole as I was, there was no way clarity would have even been an option.

"What do I do now?" I questioned.

My entire summer had been in pursuit of answers. I had searched and tried everything possible without any explanations. If nothing were actually wrong with me, what was I supposed to do to get rid of all the symptoms I was still feeling? Then a thought snuck into my head. Very subtly it inaudibly whispered, *You didn't try everything.*

My eyes grew a little wider as the surroundings started to come into focus. Looking around, I was searching every depth of thought to see if there were something I had missed, something I hadn't tried. With no luck, I dismissed the thought.

*There is one thing you didn't try!* was the next thought that snuck its way into my crumbled mind.

This time, instead of searching to find its immediate answer, I decided to just sit quietly. I decided to reflect on the thought. *One thing? One thing I didn't try? One thing? One thing ...*

*When was the last time you prayed?* the inaudible voice I heard of my mom from so many past years whispered ever so slightly as if it were a soft summer breeze sweeping across the lake.

*Prayed? Prayed? What would praying do? How could that solve anything?* I thought to myself. At this point in my life, I had left faith almost ten years prior. I knew there was a God but could really care less about Him and didn't see how He would help in any situation, especially this one.

*When was the last time you prayed?* I heard from my mom's past voice say again. No matter what I did to try to push the thought out, it was solidifying more and more. Still on my way home from the doctor's office, the thought became so constant that I couldn't ignore it.

Finally, as we were pulling off the exit, I gave in. I decided, if I were truly going to say I tried everything to get rid of these symptoms, then I needed to try everything.

I looked out the window and prayed, "God, I don't know if you are there or really how real you are, but here it goes. I have tried everything in my life to gain understanding about what is happening to me. Nothing has worked. If you are real, if you actually do care about me, I need you to come and fix all of this. I need your help. I need you to take control. Umm … Amen."

## Progress

Another week had passed since that day in the car. Every day I woke up and said that prayer almost exactly how I said it the first time. I don't know why I was doing it other than the fact that I was trying to prove to myself that I had tried everything and nothing worked, including prayer. However, something did change.

One day I woke up, came downstairs, and told my mom that I wanted to go back to my place. This came as a huge shock to me because the night before I felt I couldn't be in a different room from where my mom was in fear that something bad would happen. Now, here I was saying I wanted to go back to my place. There was just some urge in me that morning, saying that, if I wanted to move forward, I needed to move forward.

Later that day I packed up and returned home. Seven weeks from the start of this downfall, there was the first sign of progress. More signs were soon to follow.

Every day I woke up, prayed that prayer, and tried to take a little step forward. I don't know what was causing me to have this inspiration, but I wasn't stopping it. I was just trying to move forward. However, don't misunderstand the situation. I didn't just pray and everything got better. Things were still very tough, and I was still having multiple freak-outs a day. My body was still in really bad shape from basically starving myself for seven weeks, and you can imagine the state one's mind is in after going through something traumatic like that.

The one big thing that changed since that day in the car was that I had some motivation to stop searching and to instead just start living. Whatever was or wasn't wrong with me was no longer my focus. Getting my life back had become my new emphasis.

A few weeks went by, and my appetite started to return. Shortly after that, I was able to be healthy enough to start the new school year. As the weeks rolled into months, all things seemed to be slowly getting better. I still didn't even know if I believed that God were helping me, listening to me, or staying with me, but I knew I enjoyed the feeling of saying that prayer and letting out the feelings that had built up inside that I never expressed to anyone during those weeks. Most of the time, I just thought I was talking to myself.

I didn't even really know what I was asking God. "Take control of this!" That was something I saw in a movie a few times and heard others say, so I figured I should add that into my prayer.

Little did I know that I was eventually going to find out what it really meant and looked like.

## Choosing to Trust

The months rolled into a year. It had been a year since it had all started, a year since my life turned upside down, a year since I thought I would end it all before it ended me. In a year's time, I was able to regain the weight I lost and my ability to go out in public. The symptoms slowly started going away, and my freak-outs were far less frequent. I still felt the presence of many fears that developed during the dark period of my life, but they were becoming more manageable.

I ended up discovering that all of what happened that day at the gym was just because I was dehydrated and without proper food and rest. All the symptoms that followed were simply a mixture of anxiety and physically what my body was reacting to without eating while detoxing from alcohol, tobacco, and caffeine. When I thought I was making it better by trying to control it all, I was simply making it worse as my anxiety grew upon the realization of having no control. That seeking of control and feeling like I had none was what led to my freak-outs that I was finally able to understand and confirm were panic attacks.

Eventually I met Heather and found the gathering that she suggested for me. I discovered there that I didn't have to worry and hyper focus on all the things in my life. I didn't have to seek control of the things that in reality I had no control over. I looked back on the fallout over the span of seven weeks as my life seemed to get as bad as possible. I saw how it felt like God wasn't there for me. I soon realized that He was always there and was just waiting for me to stop holding on to my problems and instead give them to Him.

With the help of David's explanations and what I learned

during my time at the church, I discovered the freedom and power that prayer brought to my life. That whole time I was praying each and every day without ever thinking anyone was listening. It turns out someone actually was. It was God, and I was learning to trust Him a little more each and every day as I shared my daily burdens.

Here is an excerpt of a journal entry I later wrote reflecting on my former misguidedness and my feelings of no one listening.

*4/11/17*

*When reviewing my life over the past months, I was in awe. Back in July, I didn't have a purpose in life (to my knowledge), and my faith was simply me praying routinely to something. I had such a misguided view of faith. I was arrogant and self-centered, living in this fantasy world that I created to substitute for my life that had only grown worse throughout the years. I think around seventh grade was when I first entered. Disillusioned, disconnected, and dissatisfied with my life caused me to create how I wanted to live in my head instead of just living. I was stuck in this for so many years. I remember back when I felt like such a phony that I had to come clean about all the lies I told and lived by.*

A phrase David had preached once always stuck with me that I think sums up how I chose to pursue my struggles and worries. It was following the time on the balcony that led up to my baptism and fully following Jesus.

He said, "If you are choosing to trust God with your eternity, can't you trust God with this?"

"This" could be anxiety, depression, self-image insecurities, and so on. Whatever it was, I learned I could trust God with it. I could tell Him through prayer what was weighing heavy on my heart and soul and know that He had a plan for me and would never leave me. Prayer became such a monumental part of my life before I ever was at the church, but because of the church, I was finally able to realize it.

## The Anxiety Airplane

I don't want to mislead anyone as I close out this chapter. It can be easy to think from what has been written that everything was horrible, I prayed and followed Jesus, and now nothing is ever wrong. So often we view God as this magic genie that we can wish upon to make everything better, and when things don't get better in the time frame that we want them to, we dismiss God and everything dealing with faith.

I have learned far too many times over these past few years that oftentimes we don't get rid of certain struggles and God doesn't make them magically disappear. What He does do, however, when we have struggles is to give us situations to help us learn to overcome them while trusting Him. This has been so true in my life, and to give one of the many stories that hold true from this concept and explain why I decided to include this chapter in the book, I will close out with one final story.

As you remember, I was baptized on December 18, 2016. At this moment, I shared the very testimony that this entire chapter is based on. I explained to the entire crowd that I was choosing to trust God with my struggles and cling to the hope that is Jesus Christ. Leaving that night, I thought it marked the day my anxiety struggles were gone for good. I fully trust Jesus, I am a child of God, and nothing can ever cause me to falter. If only it were that easy.

If you grew up around church or people active in the church world, you probably have heard the saying "Life is a marathon, not a sprint." This is a common saying used in messages to describe our growth in faith. This saying rang so true in my life only a few days after my baptism. A few days after I thought I would never be anxious again and never not trust God again, I was reminded how much training I still needed.

One of the fallouts of my seven-week anxiety debacle was that I developed some irrational fears of things. It started out with me being afraid of just about everything. Slowly, however, I was able to work away some of those fears until only a few remained. One of those that remained was a fear of flying. I had never before had a problem with planes in the past, but sure enough, this fear grew deep inside my mind.

A few days after my baptism, I was supposed to fly out of Atlanta with my family and head to New York to visit relatives. I had grown super nervous about going on this flight. I won't go into all of the details around my nerves, but let's just say that I hadn't been on a plane in a long time and I was fairly convinced I was going to be crushed inside of it by the walls closing in. There was no truth to this fear, but it definitely was a fear I had.

In the days leading up to the trip, I had been praying and hoping that everything would be fine. I gave myself pep talks that I was over this anxiety thing, it was never going to affect me again, and I belonged to Jesus now. Walking to our terminal, however, I felt the panic start to take over. Just like the very first panic attack I had years before, it had shown its ugly face again.

You could imagine how discouraged I was having a panic attack after thinking I had completely beaten it with my newfound faith. *It all must have been a lie. You are a phony. You don't trust God. Do you even believe in Him?* The thoughts tormented my mind. I thought this struggle I had with anxiety would go away once I became a believer, but here it still was, showing its ugly face, and nothing had changed.

Here is an excerpt of a journal entry prayer I wrote a little bit prior to my actual baptism day that highlights these feelings I previously had and the confusion there was that they weren't going away.

*11/24/16*

*Heavenly Father, So much has happened in my life in such a short amount of time since I accepted you into my life. Why do the anxieties and fears still creep back in even though I know you are my shield and protector? Do these questions mean that I have not fully accepted you in my life? Does this show I am still lost and confused? I feel your grace all the time, but what do I do in the times where it doesn't feel as present? I know you have not left me, so why do I fear it? Please, Lord, show me the light and help me see as you see so I can do as you say. Amen.*

Well, I was about to get those questions from my journal entry answered and the doubts I had in the airport removed. I imagine that, at that very moment, God got a huge smile on his face as He probably said the words, "Nothing has changed? Oh yea? Watch this."

Among the intense crowd of people shuffling through the Atlanta airport at Christmas time was a family I believe was perfectly placed at that moment. I saw Cherry and her family.

Now Cherry was one of the first people I had ever met at the church and had been tracking with my story since I started. She was a part of the gathering I went to every Sunday night as one of their contract workers. She was always a huge inspiration to me in terms of giving me encouraging advice through my faith journey.

Now, it is easy to say that this must have been a coincidence. If you want to cling to that, I am ok with it. However, it didn't hit me as a coincidence. To me, it was a little reminder that I needed so much. I said hi to her and her family and continued to walk to my terminal. As I walked, I reflected on all the progress I had made since showing up at the church. I thought about the status my life was in before I started praying to God and how far from the person sick on my parents' couch, slowly dying, I had become.

Seeing her reminded me of all the anxiety battles I had overcome and the peace my heart received when I prayed out to

God. I didn't even realize until after the fact that, just before I saw Cherry, I prayed out to God that I was anxious and scared and that I needed Him. He didn't make my anxiety go away, but He did provide comfort for me through it with Cherry and her family.

As I got to the terminal, I sat, feeling the panic leave my body as the peace moved in. An hour or so had gone by just before we started to board the plane. The panic I once had seemed to be gone, and it looked like it was going to be smooth sailing all the way to New York. Unfortunately one more incident was to take place, and God had one more trick up His sleeve.

Sitting in the seat, the captain signaled to all the passengers that we were about to head out to the runway to take off and we needed to store all our electronic devices. Instantly I felt my soul sink into my stomach. The panic quickly made its way from my toes up to my head. It was as if the whole situation with Cherry had never happened and I was back to square one. There was no place to run, no escaping the plane, but all I knew was that I needed to abort.

Just as I grabbed my phone to shut it off for the flight with my hands trembling in terror, an alert came across my phone. It was an email, and it was titled "Baptism Video." Once again, you can chalk this up to coincidence, but I am not going that way. I had been waiting for a week to receive the video, and due to Christmas break, I didn't expect it until the New Year. However, here God was reminding me that He is there with me and I can make it through any struggle.

I sat in the chair, ignoring what the captain had said. I needed to watch that video. It was the only way I could make it through the flight. There I sat watching the video as the anxiety slipped away, the strength took hold, and the joyous tears rolled down my face. As the wheels turned faster and faster, our speed was gaining, and our chairs leaned back as the plane entered the air, I reflected on what this new path in Christ was truly about. It is the constant battle of the struggles from within that can be overcome using not my own attempts of strength but the strength of Christ.

Years later, my counselor would put this moment into words. He said, "If we do things without any fears or worries, that's not courage. That is lunacy. It is when we have the fears, acknowledge the worries, and still choose to step into the storm that courage presents itself."

That is what I do day in and day out. I still have anxiety and probably always will. I still want to control every aspect of my life. However, now instead of trying to get rid of anxiety, I just try more and more to trust God with it all. I tell Him everything that is burdening my heart. I seek His guidance as I step forward in life and know that He will never leave me. He is always there for me, providing ways through the struggles.

If you are currently struggling with something and have tried to beat it time and time again with no luck, take a second to pause and just tell God your burdens. They might not go away instantly and might never go away, like my anxiety. But you never know what He can provide during your struggle. All you have to do is stop trying to handle your own struggles and instead give them to Him. You might be surprised how He can use your struggles. I was sure about to learn that, as you will find out in a few chapters.

**Words for Thought**

*Control*

A common struggle that people can have in life is control. Well, to speak more accurately, the lack thereof control. So often we strive to feel like we have control—control of what we eat, where we live, who we are friends with, where we work, what people think of us, and so on. The list can go on and on, but the point is the same. We so often seek control. When we lack control, it can be a very scary thing.

Time and time again, we see on the news people who have lacked control. This lack of control varies from person to person. It can be the one who lacked the control of his or her anger and went and killed a bunch of people seemingly at random. It can also be the victim who lacked—rather lost—the control of his or her body and was exploited or abused. Regardless of which side of the coin you fall, lacking control can have massive repercussions on each and every one of us. This causes us to seek control.

With this seeking of control, people can often find themselves trying to control things that can't be controlled. Some of the easiest examples of this are found when people try to control other people's actions or try to control time, trying to make it either speed up or slow down. These things simply are out of our control, yet many can fall trap to the pursuit of controlling them. Those of us who do chase after this control can find ourselves deeper and deeper into a feeling of helplessness as we feel powerless.

You might be thinking that this sounds a little crazy. Why would someone try to control something he or she can't control? But it is actually a very common thing in the world today. This thing can often end up leading people into a state of anxiety. According to the Anxiety and Depression Association of America, 40 million adults, eighteen and older, are affected by anxiety or some kind of anxiety-related disorder every year. That is 18.1 percent of the US population. I am sure the number is much higher of those that are undiagnosed. The scary part of this is that, although anxiety is highly treatable, only 36.9 percent of those people seek out and receive treatment for it. This leaves almost 60 percent of people who suffer from anxiety without help.

I looked up the definition of anxiety, and it states that anxiety is "a feeling of worry, nervousness, or unease, typically about an imminent event or something with an uncertain outcome." If you scan through this definition, you can see two key words, *uncertain outcome.*

When there is an uncertain outcome, it means there is a lack of control. No matter what is done to try to control the circumstances, the outcome hangs in the balance. This sinks in anxiety for those who have this dire need to control. We want to know what happens at the end of every situation.

As I am typing this portion, my friend Marcus sent me a picture of a book that he sarcastically commented on, saying, "I wonder what this book is about?" It fits so perfectly in what we are talking about here because the title of the book was *They Both Die at the End.*

In reality, this is the one truth, the one outcome we know for each and every life. Regardless of what you believe in or how you live your life, one statistic is certain: we will all die at the end. Other than that, doesn't every outcome of every situation have uncertainty surrounding it? Why do so many people struggle then with this deep need for control and allow anxiety to take over when control is not found?

This is something I struggled massively with throughout my life and still battle with today as I write about it. It is the uneasy feeling of something imminent about to happen, as the definition mentioned. As I have tracked back through my life, I have seen full scale what anxiety has done and how it has impacted so many of my situations.

Here is a journal entry prayer that I wrote describing this very struggle of control.

*11/28/16*

*Heavenly Father, I feel I have not trusted you. One of the cornerstones of my anxiety has been trying to put together and predict the future before it happens. I understand, Lord, that this only causes me to worry and keeps me away from doing things. I need to trust you. I need your help, Lord. When you are ready for me to experience something, I know then and only then will you allow it to happen. I now need to trust in you with what I know. I feel man's never-ending struggle is to not live for himself but instead to live for you. To not think for a second that he is controlling his true path but that it is you guiding him. Bring me from the darkness into the light, Lord, and help me to entrust my life fully to you. Help me to grow stronger in faith each and every day, and bless me with patience to allow you to work. Amen.*

At the start of this book, I mentioned my desperate need for control; otherwise I wouldn't move forward. The entire premise of this book is about the battle I carried out and still fight of trying to relinquish control. If you find a relationship between my struggles with control and anxiety and your struggles, I hope this chapter helped. This was an in-depth look at what started this battle for me in the first place and what it took for me to eventually be able to write a journal entry like the one above.

Through the remaining words of this chapter, I hope I can pass on some helpful tidbits I learned along the way that have helped and continue to help me with giving up control and dealing with my struggles. Hopefully, you too can move one step closer in giving up control of the things that can't be controlled so you can experience the joys of life. Not doing this leads all of us into traps.

*Traps*

Currently, as I am writing this, escape rooms are the big fad everyone is flocking to. The idea is that you are intentionally trapped in a room with others and have to use the clues provided to try to escape. Depending on when you are reading this book could determine whether this is still the big thing.

I hope the fad has died by the time you are reading this. Escape rooms sound like the craziest idea to me. There isn't a week that goes by where I am not turning down a request to participate in one of these. Intentionally being trapped sounds horrible. I think I'll pass.

Aside from the thrill seekers and the controlled environment of escape rooms, feeling trapped or actually being trapped can be a very traumatic experience. It is the ultimate sense of not being in control regardless of what you do. That feeling can lead people to do or think about doing very erratic things they normally wouldn't do.

That was what happened when my anxiety trapped me. The thought of taking my own life seemed like the craziest idea ever before I felt trapped. However, once the claws of the trap started sinking into my ankles, the idea seemed like the most logical thing. There just didn't seem to be any way out of the circumstances I was in. Everything I had tried to do was ineffective, so drastic measures seemed like the best next idea.

Have you ever felt like there was no way out of the circumstances you were in? Maybe you are in those circumstances right now. Maybe you are in a relationship you can't seem to get out of. It could be that you are in a job that seems to have little hope of getting any better. Maybe you feel trapped by an addiction, anxiety, depression, loneliness, and so on. It can be so draining to feel trapped in a situation.

What is so hard about these situations we get in is that, by the time we realize we are trapped, it feels almost too late to do anything. Once this feeling takes over, it becomes very easy to freeze up in our lives. We can easily stop moving all together and just sit down, accepting our fate when there seems to be no light at the end of the tunnel and we are way too far from the beginning to turn around.

When you get in moments like this, there is one thing to always remember. You always have the ability to make a choice. This choice can vary depending on the circumstances that are trapping you; however, you do always have a choice. You can choose to leave the relationship. You can choose to quit the job. You can choose to put the necessary measures in place that will lead to the end of an addiction. All of these choices listed and the many more out there do come with risks and repercussions, but if you are trapped, what do you have to lose?

For those that aren't facing a physical dilemma such as the ones stated above but rather are facing internal dilemmas, you too have a choice. Now if you have depression, you can't just choose to no longer have depression. You can choose, however, to meet with a counselor, join a support group, or do what I think is the most important thing, to choose the outlook you have about your depression. Are you viewing it as something that is preventing you from experiencing life or as something that is just along for the ride? The choice of the viewpoint you have about your struggle can become the choice that leads you out of being trapped.

When I was in the deepest traps of my life, simply making choices is what eventually led me to freedom. Each and every situation that came my way, I saw the choices and simply chose the one that forced me to move forward. For weeks, I had been choosing to stay in the comfort of my parents' house, only to sink deeper into the trap. The day I woke up and chose the other option, moving back to my place, was the day I was forced to step forward with a risk that eventually became the key thing that changed everything.

If you have sunk deeper and deeper into what is trapping you, take a step back from this book for a second and assess what choices you have. You might be surprised that you possibly have been choosing the same thing over and over again, neglecting the other choice. If you have been trapped by your weight, you might have been making the same choice to eat at the same places. The choice of trying a different, healthier place has always been present. It might just be time to consider this choice. Imagine what your life could become if you decided to consider the choice you have been neglecting. If you aren't sure which choice to make, always consider choosing the one that moves you forward.

There are always ways out of the situations we get trapped in or at least ways to make it through them. That is a promise God makes to us. He says, when things test us, a way is provided for us so we can go through it. This way is almost never using our own abilities, but using God's instead. Things might not change instantly; however, things can change over time. The choices we make are the only ways to know for sure whether anything will change. One of the ways that can help us in those times of feeling trapped is the choice we can make to pray.

*Power of Prayer*

Prayer never seemed to make much sense to me. I never understood why I should do it or what good it would bring. It seemed like words I lofted into the air to someone or something that I wasn't really sure was ever there. Oftentimes prayer also seemed like an auto response one could use when he or she didn't know how to respond to something someone said. "I'll pray for you" was the common expression. I always wondered if those people ever actually did pray for the people they said it to.

Maybe this is you. Maybe you aren't sure about the whole God thing or you haven't seen a benefit in praying to Him. Perhaps you have made the same observation I have about how people always use it as a phrase and aren't too sure of the validity of their statement. It could be that you prayed for things that didn't work out for the better. Those prayers could have been about someone overcoming an illness that didn't. It could have been a prayer about a person not leaving you that did. The prayer that caused you to stop praying could have been something as simple as getting a position or role that didn't happen, and you said, "I'm done with this."

That is ok if that is you. I completely understand. If you are anything like me, the thought of prayer and why to do it was a misconception I carried for years. It wasn't until I actually saw it clearly moving in my life that I actually was able to get rid of my misconceptions and cling to the power of it.

Bob Goff, author of one of the best books I have ever read, *Love Does*, walks around every day with one of his front pockets cut out of his pants. I'm serious. He literally takes all of his pants and cuts out one of the front pockets. He says that he does this because it only allows him to hold on to a few things and forces him to let everything else go.

Using his pockets, he describes how that relates so much to our lives. We have all the things we are holding on to and the things we must let go. He wraps up this description by saying he is trying to take what he is holding onto in life from one pocket and move it to the one with the hole as he gives it up to God.

This is what we are doing when we choose to pray. We are taking the things we so badly want to control, hold on to, manipulate, fix, and so forth and are offering them up to God. Wayne Grudem says it best, "God wants us to pray because prayer expresses our trust in God and is a means whereby our trust in him can increase."

There are so many circumstances, situations, and outcomes that we have no control over in our lives. We have a choice when it comes to those things. The first option is that we can do what I did and desperately chase after them in efforts of trying to control them. We can put forth the upmost energy with little to no prevail. The other option is that we offer it up to a God who loves us, cares for us, and actually can control any and every situation. Choosing to offer it up to Him takes massive trust as you say, "I have no control over this, but you do."

You might be surprised what happens and the joy that comes when you start to take the focus off what your abilities are and start giving situations up to the one with unlimited abilities.

Don't get me wrong though. God is not a wishing well. We can't simply pray to Him and poof everything gets better. He does have the power to do that, but I don't want faith to be lost if it doesn't happen right away.

When we pray to God, like Grudem said, we are trusting and growing our trust in Him over time. By doing this, we are relieving the pain, weight, and stress that takes hold of us when we chase after control. Imagine what your life would be like if you no longer were walking around trying to keep everything floating above the water. Instead you clung to the truth that you might not have control, but someone does, and you're putting your faith in Him.

My small group, a group of guys I meet with once a week to talk about life and faith, just met last night. We have recently tried to take a more intentional approach to prayer. You could see the relief of stress, pain, depression, and so on that all of us have had since we started saying, "I'm not in control, but you are, God." None of us hoped things would get better. We just didn't really have any other options and figured we would give it a shot.

That is my challenge to you. Regardless of whether you buy in to all this God stuff or not, I challenge you to say this prayer every day for the next thirty days. What's the worst that could happen from doing this? Just give it a shot.

*Heavenly Father, I have tried so hard in life to control things, and it is wearing on me. I am starting to see that I don't have control. However, you do. Please take the things that are weighing me down (name those things) and reveal to me the desires you have put on my heart. My abilities are limited, but yours are not. Help me, Lord. Amen.*

I'd be excited to hear what you experienced during and after that time. Hopefully what is to come from this are many things, most importantly, progress.

*Win or Grow?*

When I was a kid, my most feared day on earth was the parent-teacher conference. I was the epitome of a class clown, and that was the day my mom would find out officially. Once I became a teacher, I didn't think that day would still be as monumental. I was so wrong. The day wasn't hard due to having to talk to parents. I loved and still love talking to parents. It was hard because I had to sit in agony as parents were dissatisfied with their child's performance.

Now, I am not talking about all my parents. It was more like a handful each year. The reason for their dissatisfaction was due to the results they were looking at. Many only saw the letter grade or the percentage. The one thing they weren't looking at was the progress their child made. To me, that was the most important thing.

Going from a B to an A is great. However, going from a first-grade reading level as a fifth grader to a third-grade reading level in just a few months was way more impactful. However, those few parents saw that their child still wasn't at their grade level and that wasn't ok. This often caused them to overlook all the hard work and progress that their child made. Their dissatisfaction imprinted in that child's brain, "If you aren't at this level, then nothing else matters."

We see this in many areas of life. If you ever played sports, so many team goals were and are related to winning. Not often was progress the main focus. If your team didn't win, it didn't matter that you scored your first goal. This can also be seen in certain work environments. If the client wasn't signed, then the thing was viewed as a failure. The fact that you gained experience trying to close a deal gets overlooked.

I say all of this because we are left to a choice when we go through life. The thing we must chose is whether we are going to look at the results or the progress. These might seem hand in hand; however, the mind-set that goes along with them is very different. To put it into simpler terms, are you after the win or the growth? Both are great, but if you must choose one, which is it?

It might be easy to say the win; however, let's think about it for a second. When you are constantly chasing after the win, conquering something, or gaining the position, you are left with limited outcomes. Your outcomes are that you win and everything is great or you lose and everything stinks. You might be thinking that winning provides growth, but that is not always a sure thing.

I have known many people who have won in things but didn't grow in any way. I am sure you have known people like this before. These are those people in our lives who gain so much but may not deserve it while those who do deserve it miss out. Maybe it was the person with the questionable character who got the girl or guy while the nice person didn't. This could be the person who cheated his or her way through school and got the degree and high-paying job, while the one who studied every night is jobless. Winning doesn't guarantee growth.

Now don't get me wrong. I love to win. I am often guilty of striving for it a little too intently. Also I am not on the bandwagon of twelfth-place ribbons because you showed up and breathed air. However, I have learned through the years that, when I only chase a win, any growth or progress that took place was wiped away if I didn't succeed.

I experienced this firsthand over the past few years. After high school, I put on a significant amount of weight. At one point, I weighed almost a hundred pounds more than my normal functioning weight was. For years, I tried to tackle the problem with the win-or-lose mentality. When the eating healthy lasted only a week and the gym plan was thrown away after a few days, I started telling myself I was a failure.

That is a trap so easy to fall into when it comes to our struggles. If you have anxiety, depression, weight problems, self-image insecurities, money issues, and so on and you live by the win-or-lose mentality, it can be a setup for failure. What you are telling yourself is that, if you don't conquer or beat this problem, you have failed. This then leads into you telling yourself you are a failure and causes you to give up trying all together.

Many of the problems or struggles we battle with every day might not be able to be conquered or defeated. Anxiety or depression might be something you battle against your whole life. What you can do though is progress in how you deal with it. You can make little steps forward, like hanging out with people even though you don't want to get out of bed that day. Maybe you need to go meet with a counselor every week for a while to work through your insecurities. However, that can progress into eventually only having to meet with them once a month.

Whatever it is that you are struggling with, there is hope that you can struggle with it less through progress. In my battle with anxiety, I wanted to defeat it so I never had it again. However, I soon realized that probably wasn't possible. What was likely was growing in how I dealt with the feelings of being anxious.

That is what God showed me and shows us. He reveals how much stronger we are when those struggles we have show back up in our lives after we have chosen to trust and invite Him in. We are able to see how much progress we have made since the last time the struggle showed up. As you deal with your battles and struggles, think about which mind-set you are approaching them with. Are you trying to win or grow? If you are trying to win, when you don't, you have failed. If you are trying to grow, when you do, you have the potential to win.

*Challenge*

We all have things in our lives that we will battle with. Maybe you just finished battling with something or are currently battling with something. Whatever and whenever it is, I hope that some things in this chapter can be of some assistance to you. Whether you are in church or not, your life has a trajectory. Whether you invite God in on that life or not, your ability to control things is still the same. We don't really have any.

I hope that, if you struggle with trying to control everything leading you to battle anxiety, you will start to relinquish the control and torment that fills your life. Take the risk of praying to God over the next thirty days about Him taking control. See how it affects your life and the joy that comes from putting your trust in something other than your own abilities.

Consider inviting God into your struggles. Approach them with a mind-set of growth and progress instead of conquer and defeat. You just might be blown away at how much progress you make and how much stronger you become in dealing with them.

# CHAPTER 4
# Searching for a Surrounding

I had been attending the Sunday night gathering for a few weeks at the time, and I was showing up every time and sitting in what I dubbed my seat, the last seat in the last row. It always was my escape route out of there if I decided I needed to leave. Another reason I always sat there was because I hadn't really met anyone and didn't know where else to sit.

Now, if we ever get a chance to meet, you will soon learn that I am a very extroverted person. The one exception is when I am in a new place where I don't know anyone. I instantly turtle shell and become the world's biggest introvert. I don't talk to or look at anyone. However, once I meet one person, the horses are let out of the gate, and I will strive to meet as many people as possible.

That hadn't happened yet at the Sunday night gatherings. I would show up, sit in the same seat, sing songs, listen to the message, and leave. Week after week, this was my routine. One Sunday, it dawned on me that this routine would last forever if I didn't change things up. So I decided that particular Sunday I was going to take a huge step forward, and I literally mean one step. I decided to sit in the last seat in the second-to-last row. I know, monumental. Thank you very much. The step turned out to be bigger than I thought.

Around this same time, I had met David, and we had begun our discussions of me volunteering with the high school ministry. David seemed to know everyone, and it is easy to make the conclusion that, if you were hanging out with him, you were sure to be introduced to a large quantity of people.

That particular Sunday night, I happened to see David walk in and make his way toward the front rows of the chairs. This shocked me because I hadn't seen David there before. The high school ministry he works for is finished around 6:30, and the gathering started at 7:00. It was a tight transition to make it in time, plus he usually had to meet with a few volunteers afterward. So I assumed he just went home each Sunday. This Sunday was different.

He started to walk past me as I very awkwardly, as I can recall, said "hey" to him. Stopping in his tracks for just a brief moment, he turned around, shot me an excited "hey," and kept on to his seat. Like a creepy person, I watched him every step of the way as he made it to his row. This was the only row in the whole place that was completely filled with people. I had seen them a few times before. They all seemed to know each other, and I always thought it was interesting how they gave each other the biggest hugs one would ever see.

*Of course that would be where he sat*, I thought to myself. *He knows everyone.*

I continued to watch them in mere observation as I started reflecting to myself. Thinking back to the once-tight knit group of fraternity brothers I had a few years prior, I felt a sense of sadness and loneliness weigh in on my heart. I wished I had what they had, a close friend group. I started to look away as it was starting to become painful to watch. Looking around, I was still sitting alone and figuring that, even though I moved a row closer, my row was still pretty much empty and, from the looks of things, was going to stay empty.

Just as the last thought was rolling across my mind, someone with a volunteer badge on came up to me and asked if I wanted to move closer. I looked at her in disbelief as if she had just read my every thought. I froze for a split second, seeing the large gap of rows between David and me. I weighed the odds and realized I would never be able to close that gap.

I looked at the nice volunteer and said, "No thanks."

"Are you sure?" she asked very softly with a concerned look on her face.

"I … I'm fine. Thank you though," I muttered with a tone of defeat and devastation.

She walked away, and I began to sulk. Going to this gathering was great. Clearly I was experiencing a change in my life; however, the main thing I came for was still missing. I still didn't have community. I pondered if I should keep going. It had been weeks since my first night there, and I still didn't know anyone. Every night, I sat alone, worshiped alone, and felt alone.

"Maybe this is my last night coming," I suggested to myself with a sense of failure pulsing through my veins.

"Phil! Hey, Phil!" a distant voice said.

"God!?" I exclaimed.

"Hey, Phil, up here!" the voice said again, coming into more focus. Looking over toward the direction where I heard the voice, I noticed it was David, not God. (Man, that would have made for an awesome story if it were God.)

"Phil, come sit with us."

I froze as David's arm was waving me to his row. It was the row with all the people, the friends, and the hugs. I was being called to that row. I slowly moved out of my chair. I looked back as I saw that volunteer from before, smiling back at me as she was witnessing what was happening. Giving me an encouraging nod, she watched as I turned and headed toward David.

As I was walking up to the row that was almost completely full, I felt super awkward. I knew none of these people, outside of me observing them week after week. David was sitting in the middle of them, and there seemed to be only one seat open, the seat on the end of the aisle several people away from him. What was I to do, scream across the row at him to say hi and then sit silently at the end of the row?

"Hey, guys, scoot down. Phil, right here, man," David said as he signaled to the seat right next to him in the middle of the row. I started making my way to the middle seat as the people I was passing were saying hi. One by one, David started introducing me to everyone in the row. Something was different about this meet and greet compared to others I had been a part of in the past.

Usually when being introduced to people, they would say hi, possibly catch my name, and then continue with what they were doing. This time every person paused, made clear eye contact, took a second to say something back to me, and, instead of returning to what they were doing, stayed and asked a question or two about me. It was like nothing I had ever seen before. I truly felt welcomed, and I had only just met everyone.

It is truly amazing what a simple inviting gesture to someone sitting alone could do to change the course of his or her life. That is exactly what happened when David called on me.

Here is an excerpt from a journal entry prayer I wrote around this same time, highlighting the magnitude of this moment for me.

*10/17/16*

*Heavenly Father, I moved from the back to the second row at the gathering. In tears during worship, I can't find the words to thank you. You did all of this for me. I thank you, Lord! Amen.*

## The Dinners

Following the service that night, I heard people talking about doing something when they left the church. I couldn't really make out what they were saying as it was only a few people talking amongst themselves. One of the people in the conversation was Lauren Marie. She sat next to me during the service and was by far one of the friendliest people I had ever met and still is to this day.

Going from person to person, she seemed to be helping orchestrate the plans. I was acting like I wasn't really paying attention, knowing I just met all of them and the chances of me getting invited were slim to none. Inside, however, I was screaming and begging that my name would be called.

"You coming to dinner with us?" Lauren Marie stated to me. I say *stated* because it was worded as a question but more so posed as a clarifying statement.

"Umm ... Yea, sure. What dinner?" I asked with possibly the least confident voice I had ever used.

"Every week after the service, a bunch of us go out to eat and hang. It's really one of the only nights of the week that we can all hang out, and it kind of keeps the night from ending. You know what I mean? You are welcome to join. We usually go to Marlow's," she explained.

"Sounds good to me. I'll meet you there," I stated a little more confidently.

Never in my life would I have agreed to this before. This was the type of situation I tried to avoid. I didn't really know the people. I was pretty convinced I forgot everyone's name, and now I was supposed to have an entire meal with them. It also was on a Sunday night, which was a school night for me.

*What could I have to lose? Why not take another risk?* I thought to myself, reflecting on the risk I took in showing up at the church weeks prior.

When I walked into Marlow's, I assumed there would be only a few people since it was almost nine o'clock on a Sunday night. Man, was I wrong. Recognizing some of the people I had met earlier, I located the tables—yes, tables—where I was supposed to sit. There must have been about fifteen to twenty people all sitting down and looking like they were having the time of their lives. Joining them, I was quickly introduced to just about everyone sitting there, and the night took off.

Laughter, excitement, stories, and serious conversations were all on the menu. It was like something you would see out of a movie, and if this book were ever made into a movie, this scene would be the one I would focus on the hardest to try to capture the moment and the feeling in that restaurant that night. It was as if we were all the only people on the planet and time had completely stopped.

Everyone was super polite and nice, asking me question after question and truly listening to what I had to say. We were there about two hours, and it was a night I would never forget. It was the first night I could honestly say I had found a community.

Week after week, we all would show up at the Sunday night gathering, sit together, and then go out to Marlow's. It had become the thing I looked forward to each and every week. When things were tough during the week, I knew I only had to survive till Sunday.

The best part about these dinners was that the conversations never stopped, never got boring, and never repeated themselves. If we left off on something the week prior, it would be picked right back up the second we sat down at what came to be our tables. There was no fighting. There was no rude behavior, just pure love and joy as we all experienced life together.

One thing no one could have ever guessed, especially with adding me to the invite, was that this would become a place we could all invite new people who attended the gathering or people we found sitting alone, like me, months prior. This was something I was really passionate about. I saw what life change it caused for me, and everyone was more than happy to make this a thing. Each Sunday, there was a new person.

Some nights it was a smaller crowd of ten or so, and other nights it was as large as thirty people. It didn't matter who you were or what your background was. If we saw you, you were invited. There were people at times who just overheard others talking about the dinners and showed up. We didn't care. We were so happy to see them.

The best part about the dinners was that there wasn't much of a system to them. There wasn't really someone in charge. It was just an organic thing that formed every Sunday night. No one planned anything during the week. All it took was one person to start asking the question of who was going to dinner, and the night was started.

Lauren Marie happened to be the main person who usually started the conversation. However, she went away to college a few months later, so someone else needed to sort of step in and get the question flowing around. That person turned out to be me.

Here is an excerpt from a journal entry I wrote after a follow-up dinner I had with a friend from the Sunday night dinners that I think encapsulates what they were like.

4/3/17

*We sat there for four hours while the finals for March Madness played. Everyone was focused on it while we talked all about faith. It's amazing that, as the world was going about and focusing on what it thought was important, we didn't even realize the game was on until there were eleven seconds left because of our conversation. We were cherishing the moment.*

We were simply doing what we were wired and designed to do, experience life with others. As I sought to find community, things turned into me helping others find it as well. I never thought simply going to dinner would be so impactful on my life, and I was soon to find out how impactful it was on other people's lives as well.

## Similar Roads

About six months into going to the Sunday gathering, just before she left for school, Lauren Marie convinced me to start volunteering for it. At this point, I had already been volunteering in the elementary and high school ministries and really couldn't get enough of the church. I loved being there, I loved the community of people I had met, and I was eager to see what else could possibly happen by investing everything I could there.

My volunteer role was one where I stood at this little booth that had the "Come As You Are" banner. I saw this booth my first night there with the banner hanging over it. How ironic. At this booth was where first-time attenders would go and find out more information about the gathering, other ministry areas, ways to get connected, and general information about the church overall.

I would stand there and converse with anyone who wanted to have a conversation. One minute I could be answering questions about the church; the other moment I could be hugging and praying over someone who just poured his or her heart out to me. Whatever was needed at the specific moment, I tried to provide.

So many wonderful things took place at this little booth. I remember the first time I got to pray over someone. A guy named Jason had come up to the booth one night as Mallory introduced us.

He began to tell me his story, and we hit it off right away. This was his second time coming to the Sunday night gathering, and he was describing much of what had happened to me when I first showed up—discovering the podcasts, listening and reading everything he could get his hands on, and feeling like he had found a place he could finally call home after many struggles throughout his life. The story went on and on as I stood there and smiled, fighting back tears, reminiscing on how this was literally me six months prior and thinking about how far I had come since that moment.

When he had finished his story, he started disclosing his personal struggles he was currently going through. In respect and protection of his privacy, I won't go into detail, but let's just say they were very heartbreaking to hear. I could see him holding back tears himself as sentence after sentence poured out of his trembling mouth.

The whole time I kept thinking, *What do I do? How can I fix this? What advice can I give him?* Then I started thinking about me when I was in this moment in my life. I thought about what helped me the most in that immediate time period and then in the follow-up. Something came over me that I never expected.

I had this urge to ask if I could pray over him. Prayer had been so monumental in my early struggles and had been truly life giving since. I knew I didn't have what it took to help and guide him, especially since I was just as new at all of this as the man who was pouring his heart out to me. However, there was one thing I could do: I could guide him to take all his struggles to someone who would know how to guide Jason. This was God.

That night, in the middle of all these people coming and going from the Sunday gathering, I stood there and put my hands on his shoulders as we both closed our eyes and I prayed out loud for him. I asked God to lift the burdens of his heart and to provide clarity on the path he was traveling down and the comfort to know he was not alone in his struggles. We stood there as the only two people on the earth, crying together and experiencing a moment I would never forget.

Jason started coming to the weekly dinners shortly after that night. He started building a community of his own, and he began volunteering. His story eventually started to ripple around the church about the path he had come from and the transformation God was able to bring to his life. Mallory ended up sharing his story at the church's biggest conference that took place every two years for church leaders from all around the world.

This guy who walked into an unknown place, invited in a

similar way as I was, found hope and peace from the torment of his life. The best part was that God was using someone who was previously labeled insignificant by others in such a significant way through all the lives his story touched.

I was and am so truly blessed to have been just a small part of Jason's journey to community. We still talk about the night we prayed together. Having dinner together just a few nights ago, we were talking about how much both our lives had changed after that moment. More on my change in the next chapter, but before I finish up this part, I do want to point out the greatest change that took place in Jason's life.

The night seemed all too familiar: chairs set up in a horseshoe fashion, reserved signs on a large portion of seats, and the black, rectangular object in position. This particular night, there was another baptism that was going to take place at the Sunday night gathering. It was to be the third baptism ever, and it was Jason's.

As his testimony video was shared and came to a close, I stood up with tears in my eyes, cheering louder than I had ever cheered before. The whole place was going crazy because everyone there had heard of Jason's journey at that point and was able to witness firsthand the transformation God had done in his life.

Following the moment, he introduced me to his family, and we took a picture together along with the first person who had ever gotten baptized at the Sunday night gathering, Ally. We called ourselves the Baptism Trio. Smiling like never before, we all laughed and cried, reflecting on how much our lives were changed because of a simple creation of community that surrounded us and that we could call home.

## The Next Seat

With the new year of 2017 starting, I thought it would be a good idea to try out some of the programs that the church offered.

These ranged from help dealing with money all the way to professional counseling. If there were anything that anyone was going through, there was sure enough something put in place for it. It was one of the many things I grew to love about the church. No matter who you were and what you were going through, there was always help available.

I decided to try out some of these to get a better grasp on what they were so I could better guide people to the right one they needed. First, I signed up for a financial program to better help me with my money and on how to be the best steward possible. This set me up with a financial advisor who tracked with me for a few months. It was one of the greatest things ever. To this day, I still stay in touch with my advisor now as more of a general mentor. However, I know, if I ever needed any help with financial guidance, he is just a call away.

Following the success of the financial advising, I decided to sign up for a program that helped people who were either new to faith, returning to church after a long absence, or had bad church experiences in the past. I could check off all three of those things on the list. This consisted of meeting with a group of people in the same boat as I was and walking through a curriculum with a few leaders who would help guide the conversation over a series of a few weeks. It was designed to be a place where no question was off limits and any doubts one had about faith, God, the Bible, and so on could be expressed without judgment.

I signed up because I was interested in learning more. I could have never expected some of the amazing breakthroughs I experienced. Discovering what grace truly meant, learning more about why Jesus died for the world, and experiencing the overwhelming truth surrounding the resurrection were all monumental shifts in my faith journey for me during this time.

Now if you aren't really sure about any of those things, you have doubts that Jesus is even real, or you have read tons of things pointing against the proof of the resurrection, that is ok. This story is not about proving or debating any of those ideas. Please keep reading because what this story is pointing to helped become one of the main inspirations for me deciding to write this book. What took place in one single experience during this group showed me how our lives can have major impacts on others, how God can use our stories to help those who need it the most, and how a simple gathering of a temporary community can change the course permanently of someone's life.

The 11:00 church service just let out as I gathered my things and made my way down from the balcony of our auditorium. In my hands, I had my journal that I had started bringing to church a few months back so I could take notes on what I was learning, my Bible, and the curriculum book we were going to use during this group I just joined. It was gearing toward the end of March, and I was both excited for this new adventure to start and exhausted. We were coming to an end of state testing preparations back at the elementary school where I taught.

Heading into the part of the church that was specifically designed for these groups to meet, I searched for the room we would be meeting in every Sunday for a little over an hour over the next several weeks.

Seeing Adam standing just outside the doors, I said hello to him. He was the director of this program, and it was a huge relief to finally walk into one area of the church for the first time knowing at least one person. He showed me where it was and encouraged me to know that it was going to be a great experience. Still thinking I was just there for a bit of research, I brushed off his comment as I entered the room.

Upon entering, I could see two couches, a few single but very comfy-looking chairs, a TV on the wall, and a centrally located coffee table that had some books on it. It literally looked like I wasn't in a church anymore but instead in someone's living room. When I walked in, a brief discussion was taking place among two men and two women. As soon as I entered, the conversation stopped and was followed by a very warm greeting from a guy named George, whom I had spoken with on the phone a few weeks prior; another guy named John; and a woman named Amanda. These three were the leaders of the group.

Glancing over, I remembered there were two women in the room when I first entered, but I had only met one of them. Sitting on one of the single chairs was the other woman. I had recognized her from seeing her a few times here and there at the Sunday night gathering but didn't recall if we had ever met before.

At first look, she seemed very shy and possibly unsure if she were in the right room. To help make her feel a little more welcomed, I walked over and introduced myself. This was something that became almost second nature after I had started volunteering at the gathering.

In a very soft voice, she said her name was Fefe. We started up a brief conversation about the Sunday night gathering from where we both could recognize each other from. I decided to take the single seat next to her as the rest of our group slowly trickled in over the next few minutes.

Once everyone was accounted for, our leaders kicked off the start of the group. Even though we had all introduced ourselves to each other as we entered the room, they thought it would be a good idea to go around the room, say our names, and share what had brought us to this group. I never liked these kinds of exercises since I always felt that everyone was just waiting for his or her turn and thinking about what he or she was going to say and not processing anything anyone else had said.

The leaders started us off by each saying who they were and what had led them to decide to lead this group. After they were all done, a bit of awkward silence filled the room. I wanted to go right ahead and speak; however, I had recently been working on not being the first to talk. This was a bad habit that I had picked up, which usually led me to dominating the entire conversation. If you have ever been in a group with me, you know exactly what

I am talking about. I decided to hold my tongue, feeling that it was better for me to learn how to listen first.

The first person introduced herself and described how she was there because she didn't really grow up in a faith-based household in China but was very interested in what Christianity was all about. The next to go was a couple. The wife spoke first and described how she was left with a lot of questions from the faith she learned as a child, but which were never answered. She said she was here to clear up some of those questions.

The husband went next. He stated that he was mainly there to please his wife because she felt, if they started going to church, it would help him deal with some struggles he had from his work as a former undercover cop.

I went after them, describing all my reasons for being there. A few more people went after me, sharing various reasons as to what brought them. The only one left to share was Fefe, who was sitting next to me. Looking at her, you could tell she didn't enjoy speaking in front of people and seemed to be debating whether she was going to make a run for it.

I never understood why she didn't enjoy speaking in front of people. Even to this day, it seems to be a mystery. If you ever get a chance to hear her, you will soon realize that she speaks with a beautiful accent, which we discovered was from Ethiopia. Anyways, after she told us who she was and where she was from, in the softest tone imaginable, she went on to describe what brought her to this group. No one in the room was prepared for what we were about to hear.

"I go every once and a while to the Sunday night gathering here," she began to say. "I grew up in a very orthodox upbringing, and I liked the gathering because it was very different from anything I had experienced. One night while I was there, I heard this guy talking about his life. Wait ... No, it was a video of him talking. This guy was talking about the entire struggle he had in his life, and by turning his life over to Christ, he saw that his life was never the same again. I figured, if all of that could have happened to him and he chose Jesus, then anyone could. So why don't I give it a try?"

The room was one of the quietest I had ever been in at that moment as everyone intently listened to the genuineness in her voice. Everyone was looking at her. I had just realized that I was the only one that wasn't.

I was instead looking straight ahead as tears started to fill my eyes. "Umm, Fefe. Did this guy get baptized that night?" I asked with a quivering tongue.

"Yea … Yea, he did as a matter of fact! How did you know? Were you there too?" she asked as my heart rushed with emotion.

"Umm, Fefe, that was me. That was my video and my baptism that night." I said those final words as the tears that were clouding my vision finally released like a storm moving across the water.

"Wait a minute. Wait a minute. Wait a minute." John spoke up as he waved his arms. "You mean to tell me that the reason you are here, Fefe, is because of a video and baptism of a guy that you saw one Sunday night and that very guy happens to be the guy sitting right next to you?"

"I … I guess so," Fefe stuttered to say.

"Wah—" John couldn't even finish his expression.

No one could. We all just sat back in our chairs in silence for what seemed like hours, taking in what we knew was going to be a really special group.

I looked up to the ceiling and praised God right there. I thanked Him for the life He has led me through. I thanked Him for taking my struggles and my story to help someone else's life. Most importantly, I prayed for Fefe that she would find whatever it was that she was looking for during this group.

As the weeks rolled through, we all enjoyed great discussions, laughter, shared doubts, questions, and so on. Fefe had some of the greatest doubts and questions. You could tell there were things inside that she couldn't seem to find peace from when it came to faith. However, we were there for her every step of the way. Even though it was a community for just a short period of time, it was a place that each and every one of us knew we were wanted, we were welcomed, and we could call home.

Here is a note I wrote down during that time period of something the lady from China said that I thought was so powerful while we were all meeting.

*4/2/17*

*"I realized I needed to depend on someone for my life and I am not dependable, so I relied on Jesus," stated Sherry.*

The last week of the group came, and once again, we all sat around in our chairs and had one final chance to share. Our leaders asked us what our plans were once we left this group and if there were any way they could help guide us in the direction that we were heading. Around the room, each person shared his or her final remarks until it got to Fefe. Once again, she was the last one to share, and she was going to give us one more surprise.

Looking around at everyone and then finally landing her eyes on me she said, "I think … I think I want to look into baptism. Philip, would you help me with this?"

My heart fell to mush on the floor as I was trying to process the words that were just spoken. We all were having a hard time believing what we heard. Here was someone who seemed to have more doubts as the weeks went on, and now as her closing statement, she said she believed. To top it all off, she asked me, of all people, the guy who was so lost in the world less than a year ago, to help walk with her through the process.

I hugged Fefe as tears rolled from my eyes, and we walked out of the room for the final time together, talking about next steps.

It's been a little over a year now since that moment in the room, and it still brings my heart so much joy. Fefe and I stayed in touch here and there in the following months. However, due to both of our busy schedules and some unforeseen things, it grew harder and harder for us to keep in contact. It is sad to write that I haven't had the pleasure of seeing Fefe share her public profession of faith and get baptized. For some, the journey can be a very long one with many turns, but I never lose hope.

It is easy to dismiss the story because it didn't end with her getting baptized, but that was never the point of the story, and I think that's what makes the story so real. The purpose was never about a glamorous ending but instead about how one story can influence and become part of someone else's story through community.

After rereading the words I just wrote of the story Fefe and I shared together, I said a little prayer that hopefully I will get to one day see her make the amazing decision. Fefe, I am here when you are ready.


**The Doorbell**

Around the same time that Fefe and I walked out of the room together, summer was starting. There were some very exciting things on the horizon that you will read about in the next chapter. Along with those exciting things, there was one thing that I never could have expected and never thought I would be able to handle. I chose this last story not only because of where it fell on the timeline of my first year at the church, but mainly because I think it sums up just how important and impactful community is in our lives.

This whole chapter—really this whole book—has been about how much my life was forever changed once I started attending church and the people who helped me along the way. From some of the first people I met attending the Sunday night gatherings to those I met volunteering in the high school and elementary ministries and the people I connected with at the dinners and elsewhere throughout my time at the church, God was about to bring all of them together in this one moment in time.

The date was June 15, 2017, and it was the day my father died suddenly. Darkness took over my world that once seemed to become so bright. I felt abandoned and alone on this earth without him. A million questions were racing through my mind in the immediate fallout. *What am I going to do? Who is going to give me advice when I need it? Who is going to teach me how to be a husband and a father?* Question after question poured out of me as silence swept across my life related to getting any answers.

The doorbell rang. It was David and my buddy Adam (not the same Adam from before). Adam was a guy I met the first time I observed the volunteer position at the high school ministry. You might remember his name when I thanked him in my baptism testimony. They walked in the door of my parents' house, moments after my life had the bottom ripped out of it.

My face was a mix of red puffiness and agony from the hours of crying. Both gave me huge hugs, and we sat down in the living room. What seemed like days passed as we sat there and chatted about everything. One thing I was explaining to them was how Amy and Erinleigh, two people who worked for the church in the elementary ministry I volunteered for had just left. They had been with me for hours following the initial discovery of my dad's death. The loneliness and abandonment I was feeling was taking a pause while they were there.

David asked if I wanted to get out of the house for a little while and drive around to help occupy my mind. I agreed, and we drove around for a while, leading us to eat at one of my favorite places. While we were there, they tried to do anything they could to help remind me they were there for me and that I wasn't in this alone without coming right out and saying it. They showed me funny pictures they had on their phones and retold stories we shared through the year together. And every once in a while, it grew quiet. Each time the quiet fell on the table, they would look at me and smile. This smile, I could see said very clearly, "We are here for you."

Following the restaurant, we all grabbed some ice cream. While there, my phone rang. The call was from Darren, the high school ministry director I had met quite a few times through my volunteering. He talked to me for a little while. There was one thing he said in our conversation that still sticks with me to this day.

Upon his many condolences, he shared a bit of truth and hope as he said, "Normal as you know it is gone. However, you will find a new normal. Finding your new normal is what the grieving process is all about."

Following that truth, we got off the phone. Finishing up our time together, David and Adam dropped me back home and headed out. The loneliness and abandonment hit play again as I started to collapse in pain. The doorbell rang again. It was a summer intern from the church that had driven over two hours in traffic to provide my family with a meal that night so we had one less thing to worry about. I had never met or seen this person before, but she was told what happened, and she delivered.

Once again, the pain was put on pause. My family sat around the house, eating little bits of the meal. There wasn't much said as we felt a long road ahead of us. The first day ended, and I already could see the presence of the people God had put in my life. I had no idea that was just the beginning.

The doorbell rang. It was two days later, and all of our relatives started filling the house for the gathering we had before the service. With my mom being one of ten, our house was slowly starting to fill up. It was great being around family, but I couldn't help but feel an emptiness in me. The life I was charging after in the church seemed unstoppable, but here I was, stopped dead in my tracks.

*Is it all over?* I thought to myself.

The doorbell rang. Some of my friends whom I met volunteering at the high school ministry had arrived. The doorbell rang. Amy, who was there two days prior, was back with her fiancé, Stephen. The doorbell rang. Some more staff members from the church's elementary ministry were here. The doorbell rang, and it was Micah and Ashley. The doorbell rang. It was Darren. The doorbell rang. The doorbell rang. The doorbell rang. There wasn't but a few seconds in between each time the doorbell rang. Our house was being flooded with people. Every time it rang, the same phrase could be heard throughout the house. "Philip, it's for you."

Friends and friends and friends kept showing up. Some of these people I had only known for a month or so while some just a little longer. Aside from my family and my fraternity brothers who were there, none of these people I had even known a full year. Here they were, over an hour away from their homes, at my parents' house showing their support. Their presence didn't make the pain go away. It did, however, make the pain bearable.

I stood there in my kitchen as I watched people from my past interacting with persons from my present. Tears constantly rolled down my face as I witnessed all of these people from the church—staff, volunteers, and friends—all there to provide comfort, support, and any helping hand that my family needed.

In the days and weeks to follow, every single day someone came to our house from the church, rang the doorbell, and provided my family with meals. When we asked how long they would do this, they always replied that they would do it continuously until we told them to stop. Even summer interns from the elementary ministry came by just to spend time with my mom. Every day the only smile I saw creep through my mom's pain was when that doorbell would ring. It always represented another person from the church.

There are only brief moments where we ever discuss anything from that day. However, there is one thing that comes up time and time again, the people from the church. My mom mentioned to me the other day that we would have never survived that moment if it weren't for all the support the church and everyone I had met there provided. She smiled and laughed as she said that all those people were there for me. "They were there for you," she constantly repeated. She gave me a huge hug and is forever grateful that I found this place. Numerous extended family members have said the same words.

I believe in those moments that God was pointing out the endless community I have gained that will be there no matter what. They are there for me in my brightest times of baptism and my darkest times of death. Never could I have imagined that I would have met all those people and that they would come through when I needed them most. Never did I realize the deep sense of belonging I sought after for so long. Thankfully, God knew. This reminder came every time the doorbell rang.


## Words for Thought

*Community*

I am currently on vacation as I write this portion of the book. While here, I wanted to make sure I didn't miss church. So this morning I loaded up my laptop, connected it to the TV in the condo I was staying in, and watched the service from my church back home. I know, five heaven points for me for watching church while on vacation. Thank you very much.

Anyways, we are doing a series right now, talking about the things we desire that other people have. Regardless of how our life is going, we often desire things that we see others are experiencing in their lives. This got me thinking on this calm night as I listen to the waves roll in that a very common sought-after thing in life seems to be community. So many want the collection of people that they honestly say is for them and with them, the group that, regardless of the time of day, they can call to chat, hang, or be there when they are in need.

So many people don't feel they have this community, but through the blessings of social media (said sarcastically), we see everyone else obviously has it, which can cause us to want it so badly. This rang so true for my life. It is one of the things that led me to the church in the first place, aside from the pretty girls.

This book started off with me describing the deep loneliness that had taken hold of my life. This was the loneliness that seemed to control every thought in my mind. When looking back on my life, it seemed that this loneliness was all too present in almost every stage of my life. Wherever I seemed to go, whatever I seemed to do, one thing always remained the same, this sense of feeling like I was doing it all by myself.

When we look at a snapshot of our current circumstances, oftentimes we judge what we see based on the people we are connected with in our life at the time. If we have a large friend group, a relationship, or a place we can call home, it doesn't matter what we are going through. Life seems pretty good. However, when one or all of those things are absent, we could have the best job in the world, the greatest salary, and the strongest outlook on life, and it will still come up with us feeling like a failure, isolated, and unwanted. When loneliness sinks in and the lack of community seems present, it often seems as if it will never end.

In previous chapters, I shared little bits about how my community came about once I started going to the church. However, to truly do it justice, portray the impact it has had on my life, and show how the local church can be the ultimate solution of community, I wanted to write a chapter specifically highlighting it. I hope something in this chapter has helped you find or grow your own community. One of the easiest ways to do that is by a simple invite.

*Invite*

"I never have anything to do," said my friend.

"Why do you think that is?" I asked.

"I don't know. I hate that I always have to call people to hang out," he continued.

"Well, have you been calling people?" I asked.

"No," he said.

This is a conversation I had with a buddy while I was writing this chapter. I couldn't help but laugh when we had this conversation that was supposed to be very serious. I'm laughing right now as I'm trying to type. It is so funny to me because it seemed then and now that he is the solution to his problem. If he never has anything to do, is always the person who has to call people to hang, and isn't calling, call someone!

Situations like this happen more often than you think. Maybe you can relate to having a similar conversation as this one with someone. We sit around wanting things to do and people to hang with, but we don't do the one thing necessary to initiate it. We don't invite people. Sitting around expecting the phone to ring or the text to come through is a waste of time. If you want something to do, just invite someone.

That was a struggle I had for years. I remember having a very similar conversation as the one above with my mom.

She told me, "Some people receive the calls, and some people make the calls. If you aren't receiving the calls, guess which one you are?"

Never have wiser words been spoken to me.

As I sat each week in the last row, I expected people to flock to me and my community to form. Now I did luck out with David and Lauren Marie inviting me to sit and eat, but it took way longer than it should have. I had been watching that group for weeks without so much as a peep to them about hanging out. If I would have taken the advice from my mom and asked to sit with them, maybe I wouldn't ever have had to consider not coming back to the gathering. They showed me that an invite never hurts.

When you find yourself feeling like you don't have a community around you, think about how much inviting you are doing. You might be surprised that it is not a lot. There are tons of opportunities out there to invite yourself into an already existing group. People have always frowned upon those who invite themselves, and I understand. There are certain limitations to it. Don't go around inviting yourself to vacations or weddings that you aren't invited to.

However, if you know some people going to the movies, assume they forgot to ask you and inquire if you can go. It is up to them to say yes or no. Don't feel bad inviting yourself. Those of you who are reading this that fall on the other side of the situation where people are always inviting themselves, you can say no. It might sound harsh, but it is even worse to keep saying yes when you don't want them there. I'll talk a little bit later about why you should say yes.

If inviting yourself hasn't worked out or seems too intimidating, that is ok. What you can do instead is invite individual people to the group you are forming. Find one person that you think you might get along with and ask him or her to coffee. If the person says no, move on to the next individual. For safety, don't do this to random people walking down the street. Please only consider those in a safe environment or ones that you are acquaintances with.

Once you get one person to say yes, you can start to invite others to coffee, lunch, dinner, and so on. That is how the Sunday night dinners started. One person invited another, and in a matter of a month or so, twenty to thirty people were coming. To Jesus juke you, that is how Christianity formed. Jesus walked up to some fishermen and said to come hang with Him. Well, he actually said "follow Him," but I like to imagine they hung out. Those men turned into twelve men, which two thousand years later has turned into 2.3 billion people. (And that is only counting those alive on this earth right now.)

A simple invite can go such a long way and have a tremendous impact on your life. Imagine what your life would be like and the joy that could arise if you stopped waiting to be asked to join a community and instead took initiative to invite yourself. Each one of us has the ability to join or create a gathering around us. It can vary from a dinner to a movement. It all starts with an invite. The invite doesn't just have to impact and benefit you. It can lead to tremendously impacting someone else's life as well.

*Impacting Others*

Last summer, the elementary ministry I volunteer for did a summer series all relating to heroes. The greatest part about this series was not the encouraging of kids to be like superheroes. The world does that enough. Instead it was all about using the powers each one of us has within to do great things in the world. There is something in this elementary lesson that we can all take away. We all have a power.

The power that we have in each of us is the power to impact others. We can impact others in a positive or negative way. The choice is up to us. It is not always the easiest choice, but depending on which you choose, it can be the choice that changes someone's life.

My friend Tyler had just come back from a baseball game yesterday where the power of choice came into full view. He told me about a foul ball that was hit into the stands, forcing people to race over to where it landed. Among the group of people trying to get the ball were a young boy and an older man. Guess who got the ball? If you guessed the man, you are right. Guess what the man did with the ball? If you guessed that he gave it to the boy, you are wrong. The man decided to keep it!

Tyler continued to go on a rant about how that guy didn't know the unwritten rules of catching a foul ball when a kid is around. If you don't know what it is or you are the guy from this story, you give the kid the ball! I know this is a silly story, but it is such a simple representation of the power we so often overlook when it comes to affecting others.

That could have been the boy's very first baseball game. It could have been the one thing the boy came to the game for. All the man had to do was take his mind off himself, and he would have seen how he had the power to make the little boy's day. What if the boy received the ball, which then led him to pursue baseball? Following that, what if it led him to become a professional baseball player?

The example can seem like a stretch, but the truth is that we don't know. None of us will know the full impact of our actions on others. All we know for sure is that there will be an impact. As we approach situations in life where we have to choose to use our power of impact, let us always choose that which benefit not ourselves but others.

I don't know if praying over Jason that night is one of the things that led him to accept Christ in his life. What I do know is that I had the power to possibly impact his life. I could have simply listened to his story, said it was great, and sent him on his way. It would have been easy to do. I had been at the church all day, I was super tired, and I had to get home.

Those are all things that would have benefited me. If I were looking for my benefit in the situation, I would have found it by leaving the situation. However, we need to look for the benefit of others in each and every situation. You might just be surprised at how much you benefit by this outlook.

Jesus tells us that there isn't any greater love than the one who lays down his or her life for others. He did that very thing for us. When you put others first in your mind, your heart, and your life, that is love, and Jesus displayed it in the most ultimate way.

Knowing He had the power to impact the world in a positive way by taking to the cross, he chose not to run and save himself. His actions instead saved the whole world.

When you see people sitting alone, like I was in the back of the room, chose the power you have within and invite them to sit with you. When people are not getting invited to things, choose the power you have within and start inviting them. If those people who aren't getting invited aren't your favorites or might be a little on the interesting side, consider that it is about what is best for them and not yourself. You have the power to possibly be the thing that changes their life circumstances. You might be surprised that those people who you took a chance on are often the ones that are there for you when you need people the most.

*Support*

Today I had to take a friend to get an outpatient surgery done. As we were driving there, silence filled the car. I could tell he was a little nervous whether he would admit it or not. He had asked me the day before if I would take him. His request sounded as if he really needed someone to be there for him. My assumptions about this were later confirmed when he finished his surgery.

He looked over at me as the doctor was finishing the final instructions of his discharge from the facility. "Thank you, man, for coming. I really didn't have anyone else to ask that would be here for me," he said in a very soft tone.

I followed his statement with the reassurance that I would always be there for him. You could tell that was a very important thing he needed to hear. That is a thing that all of us need to hear. We need the confirmation that people will be there for us when times become the toughest. The lost job, the financial struggles, the sickness, the crisis, and so forth that kicks us down in life are all the moments where we realize we can't do this life alone.

I experienced this firsthand when my dad died. The full feeling of pain stomping on me kept destroying any hope I had of being able to survive the event. That was the moment when I looked around for anyone and everyone who could possibly be available to support me through it. Without their support, I would have never made it.

This is one of the greatest benefits of surrounding ourselves with others. They are there for us and with us through whatever we face. These people we invite into our lives don't have to become our best friends and may not be in our lives for more than a moment. However, whoever they are and however long they are present is exactly the amount of time we need.

This was something I learned through the temporary group I was in. We were all together for only a few weeks, but when my life came crashing down, George was there for me. During the time when the doorbell kept ringing, I was stopped in my tracks when I saw the various people who showed up who had been absent from my life for years. They were all there when I needed it most.

One of my early editors of this book wrote a comment next to a statement I made about us all being wired to experience life with others. His comment stated that it would be nice if there were some data to support the statement. I completely understood what he meant by it but wasn't sure if I had the time to gather the data I needed to prove my case. Instead I decided to remove the line.

After writing this portion, I realized that I don't need the data to support the statement. All I need is a question I want to ask each and every one of you. Think about the lowest moments of your life. Would they have been easier or were they made easier by having others there to support you? I'm going to make a bold statement and say that it is always easier when we are surrounded by others in our darkest times, proving that we are wired to experience life with others.

*Challenge*

Life can be filled with a lot more joy when we are connected with others. The communities we join and help create have the ability to impact other people's lives and help us during our darkest times. We can form these communities or join them by inviting others in or inviting ourselves. This will cause us to stop thinking about ourselves and put others first. Taking actions as such can have the power to change the trajectory or circumstances of someone else's life.

If you currently are not satisfied with the community you are in or feel you are not a part of a community at all, the steps are simple. All you have to do is allow yourself the ability to let others in, and you will soon see them let you in. Take the risk of going where you haven't gone before, saying yes in situations you always said no to (healthy ones, that is), and allow God to guide you. You just might be surprised where you end up and the people who surround you. That's the essence of this whole chapter. I was simply searching for a surrounding, and I found it. You can too.

# CHAPTER 5
# Reaching Out in Faith

After going to the church for a few weeks, I still didn't feel I had a place where I was truly wanted. One could say the school where I worked, but they were paying me to be there. Another could say the Sunday night gathering, but this was before I made it to the second row and met people. At this time, I was showing up to a building that was filled with tons of people, listening to a message, and leaving, feeling like no part of the church was mine. This all changed the second I signed up to get involved and volunteer.

Due to coaching high school lacrosse when I was in college and once I started teaching full time, I developed a love for working with high schoolers. This made it so easy for me to want to start volunteering in the high school ministry when I first heard about it.

I wanted to be a small group leader. Just like the small group I have, the high schoolers also have their own based on their age and gender. They meet with a few leaders following the high school message each week talking about God, faith, and life. The coolest part of them is that the groups were together from freshman through senior year.

I wanted to volunteer in that position but was not able to because all the spots were filled. Secretly I think maybe it was because they knew I wasn't ready. However, I was given a position that consisted of me gathering a few seniors together and having them stand outside the doors of the church entrance where the high schoolers walked in. We would give them the biggest welcomes possible so each and every student felt that he or she was wanted there.

Looking at my position, you might think it was a huge step down compared to being a small group leader who tracked with the same group of students all four years of high school. I never saw it that way. I was just so happy that I had a place that wanted me and that I could help be a part of. I loved every ounce of my position. Watching students look up from their phones (which can be a rare sight) as a smile formed slightly across their faces from the warm welcome were some of the happiest times I have ever experienced at the church.

The best thing about my position was that it only took place for about twenty minutes before the service, which freed me up to volunteer in a bunch of other roles for the high school ministry. I literally showed up every week and asked how I could help. I had what seemed like a million little volunteer roles.

I helped out with students who were there for the first time by connecting them with the people who would get them registered in the church's system. Then if they didn't know anyone, I would be his or her best friend. I would hang out with them the whole first time they were there so it didn't seem as scary and intimidating with all the others in attendance. One or two of the students even hung with me week after week until they felt comfortable enough to hang with their small group.

Sometimes I was part of the volunteer team that met with the new students after the first message to explain a little more about the high school ministry and answer any questions they had. Another role I did was take people who were interested in volunteering with the high school ministry on a tour around when all the staff was busy. I would explain more about the various volunteer positions. There were even times I helped throw things out on stage when they were shorthanded. Two different times,

I even was the DJ alongside another high school student for the opener of events they were having.

It didn't matter what it was. I would just do it. I loved how I was able to be a part of something bigger than myself, be able to connect with others, and have a place where I felt welcomed. It became a place I could call my own, which led me to constantly want to keep volunteering. It was the greatest opportunity ever.

Each and every week, I got to roam the halls before the service. I would be hanging out and connecting with students and other volunteers. I had the privilege to sing, dance, and worship alongside some of the most spiritually driven teenagers I have ever met, and I was able to sit in on various small groups. I did this when all my volunteer roles were done, as they discussed the struggles and triumphs of their daily lives. These were some of the most prosperous times for me.

Here is part of a journal entry prayer I wrote around the same time this all took place.

*10/17/16*

*Heavenly Father, Thank you for being my guiding light and helping me see what the whole purpose of being on this planet is. I've been feeling like I missed out on so much precious time with you and others. I ask that you help me make up for all the lost time by guiding my relationship each and every day. I hope, pray, and beg that I never give up on you again and that I see everything and everyone in this world coming from your graciousness. Lord, yesterday was one of, if not the most, amazing days ever. I completely felt you through me as you pushed me out of my comfort zone into unchartered waters. I prayed that you would be my shield, and instantly I felt so much of your love and comfort. I was able to talk to complete strangers at the high school ministry and get them fired up about worship. I was in the very front, stretching my arms to you, giving you all the praise I had. Amen.*

**Engaging Environments**

One day, David and I were walking over to where we fed the high school students dinner each Sunday night. We walked past this huge entrance that was just simply magical. There were lights blinking, two large signs hanging on the walls opposite of each other with a really cool logo lit up on them. There were pillars of light beaming from the floors onto the brick columns that had pedestrian signs mounted to them. Along with that, there were three sets of double doors covered in glass that one could look through and see the ultimate child wonderland. I froze.

As I read the sign "Kindergarten–5th Grade," my eyes blew up in wonder. I turned to David and asked, "Is that an elementary school that the church has, and if so, how do I get a job there?"

He turned to me and laughed as he explained that this part of the church was where the elementary ministry took place. And then he continued walking to our destination. Falling back a little to just take it all in, I made a mental note to look more into what this ministry was all about. Then I rushed to catch up to him.

A few weeks later, I finally had the time to find out more information about the kids' ministry. My heart was full as I gained insight into what it was all about. I could tell the key mission of this ministry was wanting to make the most engaging environment possible for kids. This was my approach on teaching, so I was hooked. It only made sense that I help out in the kids' environment here as well. I signed up for a volunteer position right away. I was interested in one of the stage positions I had read about that involved a lot of energy, pumping the kids up, and playing fun games with them.

It was around Thanksgiving at this time, and I was at a Friendsgiving chatting with my friend Mary Kate, who already served in the elementary ministry, about my interest in volunteering. She suggested that the next Sunday I come be a fill-in small group leader with her. Her other leader was out, and after the service, we could try and find the production people for me to discuss a potential role.

The Sunday came where I got to see the elementary ministry in action for the first time. No words could ever describe the feeling I had seeing it all unfold. I was helping Mary Kate with her small group of kindergarteners as we sang, danced, played games, and witnessed an amazing Bible story acted out live. I was able to see a girl named Deena on stage in the position I was hoping to volunteer for, and she was amazing.

After watching her performance, I was eager to find the production people and get started. Mary Kate and I were able to track down the production director named Erinleigh. I set up a time to audition, thanked her and Mary Kate, and left super excited.

I auditioned for the stage position, got it, and started volunteering the very next week. Every single time I hopped up on the stage in front of the two hundred-plus first and second graders, I knew I was in the right place. Watching little kids be excited at church and wanting to be there was something I never had seen before and knew it was something I wanted to continue pursuing. I was able to help be a part of creating a fun environment at the church just like I could create in my classroom.

I expected that being on stage would be super fun and life giving. I got to watch each and every kid's reaction in real time to what was happening, the Bible stories we were acting out, the songs we were singing, and the fun games we were playing. What wasn't expected was how life giving all of the time off the stage and out of the spotlight was going to be for me as well.

It took a whole team of volunteers having the same passion as myself to be able to pull off the production that we did every single week. This team became such a family while we were volunteering together. When I would walk in for rehearsal, I would see Tom, Josh, and Ryan chatting and catching up on the week while preparing for the production. Chris would be on stage talking to Courtney, who was at the front of house, about some transition cues as they joked around. Chanika would be practicing with Anna, Carolyn, and Daryl as they laughed and encouraged each other. Then there was Caleb, who was in sixth grade at the time and my best pal on the team. He would be waiting on me to arrive to give me a huge "What's up, Philip?" followed by us working out what the game we were playing entailed. We also looked at what silly costume I would be in that week. Those were some of my favorite moments.

Following rehearsal each week, we would all gather together. Ryan talked us all through how the production was going to look to make sure we were all on the same page. What came after that was what I looked forward to all week long and what solidified to me the power of serving with others.

We would all go around the room and catch everyone up on anything important, urgent, happy, or sad that had taken place in our lives since the last time we all were together as we offered up prayer requests to and for each other. These moments were so powerful because we all walked together through each other's lives during the greatest moments, which we had plenty of, and some of the most devastating ones, which you couldn't even imagine.

Sitting there, watching all the laughter and tears, made me just think every single time how grateful I was and how amazing it was that God had taken a simple thought of wanting to create a fun environment for kids and formed an incredible environment around me to do just that.

When it was all said and done, we would pray together, get to our positions, and put on the most engaging environment ever.

## Changing Paths

We often want to know what is next in our lives, what we need to prepare for, and where our focus should be. This reigned so true for me throughout this entire journey. So much was happening as I was getting involved more and more, but I wanted to know what it was all leading to.

Here is a journal entry prayer I wrote as the 2016 year was starting to come to a close, asking those very questions.

*11/26/16*

*Heavenly Father, What you have done in my life and with my life in these past few months has been so amazing. You have completely reshaped my mind, the way I see the world and people, the way I view myself, and how I handle situations. No words or actions could ever show you, Lord, how thankful and grateful I am. Over these past two months, since deciding to get baptized, I have been prepping for this moment and have grown so much in my faith. However, what is next for me, Lord? Where will you lead me after December 18? What should I start prepping and planning for? Is there a heartbreak I need to prepare for? Where will I go with my job and my aspirations of ministry? I have endless questions, Lord. I trust in you and put all my hope and faith in you, Lord. I will go where you lead me. Only let me see as far as you want me to see and help give me patience to let you do your work, Father. Amen.*

Well, God was about to start forming the answers to all those questions. As the new year of 2017 had just rolled in, the high school ministry was having an amazing event where thousands of high school students gathered, worshiped, and experienced authentic community with each other for one entire weekend. I was able to be a part of it, and words cannot even describe how amazing it was.

As the final note was strummed on the guitars and the last lyric echoed across the room to finish out the weekend, all of the students started making their way to the exits to go back to where they were staying. I was walking out as well when I ran into a friend of mine, Adam.

He gave me a huge hug as he did with every single person, regardless of if he knew him or her. We got to chatting and catching up on the weekend and how his group was doing. Then a girl named Hannah walked up to us. She said "hey" to Adam and myself. I had known her from the welcome team that I was a part of with the high school ministry. She was one of the best students on it.

"Hey, Adam, are you coming to speak at our FCA next week?" Hannah asked.

"Of course. I can't wait," Adam replied.

"What is FCA?" I asked, very confused.

"It stands for Fellowship of Christian Athletes. We have it every Friday morning at our school. Actually a lot of high schools have it," Hannah explained.

"And speak there? What do you mean?" I directed my question at Adam as he said that was what he was doing.

"Basically you prepare a ten to fifteen-minute message and go and deliver it to high school students," he answered.

"What kind of messages?" I continued to inquire.

"Sermons just like here at the church, only much, much shorter," he said as he started laughing.

"Oh, that sounds really cool," I replied as I pondered on the words.

"You know, you should come speak at our FCA too. I'm on the leadership team there, and I think you would be great," Hannah suggested, looking at me with a huge smile.

"Umm … ok … sure. What do I talk about?" I asked with shakiness in my voice as I was still trying to piece together this whole conversation. Saying yes was so ingrained in me by this point. I never really was processing what I was saying yes to a lot of times.

"Whatever you'd like. I've got to run to catch up to my group.

I'll send you the date, and I can't wait. You are going to do great," Hannah said as she ran off to meet up with her friends.

Adam also had to run but wanted to make it very known to me before he left how excited he was about all that had just happened. He gave me a huge hug and said he couldn't wait to hear my message. Then he ran off.

In complete awe and excitement, I sped out of the building that night, eager to get working on a message.

## Clear as Day

I worked on the message for weeks. I wanted it to be perfect and inspiring. I wanted to take all I had experienced and learned and use my teaching abilities to help those high school students who would be in attendance.

One day I was talking about the upcoming speaking opportunity when one of my lacrosse players overheard me. He asked if I were speaking at an FCA. I told him I was, and then he told me that this school, the one where I coached, also had an FCA and a decent amount of the team already attended. He suggested that I also come and speak at their FCA. I said yes.

The FCA for the school where I coached actually was going to be before the one Hannah asked me to come speak at, so this moved up my preparation timeline a bit. However, I made sure I was ready. The news spread to the whole team that I would be speaking at their school in early March, and most said they wouldn't miss it.

Finally the day came; however, I was still just as nervous as when I was asked. I invited a group of friends to come along and hear the message at the school to help calm my nerves and provide support, especially if I totally bombed it.

Sitting in my car, looking over my notes one last time, I closed my eyes and asked God to please use me somehow. I opened the door, feeling the cool end of winter air hit my face as March rolled in. With my Bible in my hand, I stepped out and walked into the school theater with my friends.

The message I decided to go with was the story from chapter 3 about my struggle with anxiety and how prayer literally saved and changed my life forever. It was the first time I had ever publicly shared those events that took place. I'm so glad I did. Most of my players were sitting in the crowd as I got to give a little insight into my past, the roads I'd struggled down, and how God had brought me to where I was that day. Several of my players were not followers of Jesus so it warmed my heart that they were still there to show their support

It was mostly a blur following the message. Some people came up as I was walking out and gave encouraging words. My friends gave me huge hugs as always and gave some more encouraging words. Among those friends in attendance was David. He now got to see the full benefit of the impact he had made on my life as I helped try to impact other lives.

As everyone said their goodbyes, I got in my truck and checked the time to see when I had to be back at the elementary school. I had taken a half-day to be able to speak. Closing the car door, I sat in silence as I heard the engine rumbling under the hood. The subtle vibrations of the truck were felt as it quaked in its stationary position in the parking lot of the school. I pondered over what just happened—the feelings I had as I prepared the message, the freedom and joy I felt when delivering the message, and the wholeness and completion I felt after the message was over.

I looked out the window. "God … I think … I was …" I said, pausing to try to process the words that were pouring from my heart onto my lips. "I think I was meant to do that for the rest of my life."

It was there clear as day, a path I had never imagined that was just laid out in front of me. I had never felt so strongly about something before in my life. There wasn't a single presence of doubt in my mind. I knew right then and there that I was meant to communicate the good news of Jesus Christ to people for the rest of my life.

## Taking the Risk

The rest of the month of March was simply a blur. A mixture of pure shock from the realization that I had in the truck, being completely burned out from all of my over commitments that were starting to catch up with me, and test prepping my students for the state standardized tests had me in survival mode. There was an end in sight though. Spring break was coming up.

Never in my life was I more excited but also nervous for spring break to come. This wasn't because I had any vacations planned. I was excited because of what spring break was going to result in and nervous because of what was going to result from spring break.

Teaching contracts for the next school year were sent out the week before spring break. I knew that I needed to take the entire spring break to figure out what my plans were for the next year. Was I staying where I was, or was I possibly going to try to pursue a career in ministry?

To add just a little context to this moment, I had been considering leaving teaching and doing something else for a little over a year. I just never knew what the "something else" would be. Once the church came into the picture and with the revelation I had in my truck, the fogginess was starting to subside.

My whole life, I wanted to be a teacher. I remember playing school when I was a little kid to a degree higher than most real teachers did as their job. I student taught from the time I was seventeen, completed four years of undergraduate studies, worked three years as a full-time teacher, and received a nomination for teacher of the year. Was all of it coming to an end? As hard as it was to believe, I felt like my heart and passions were aimed everywhere else and not on my classroom or my career as a teacher.

I reflected on my experiences at the church up to that point. All I wanted to do was create engaging environments where I could talk about Jesus all day long. It seemed the clear calling, the main calling that had formed, was to do that through the local church in full-time ministry.

I decided to take the risk of a lifetime and make 2017 my last year as a teacher. I would apply to work at the church that created the platform for me to discover Jesus and all of His love so I could help others have the same experience I had.

## The Call

My decision to leave teaching was met with many questions.

"You did what?"

"You're going to work where?"

"Are they hiring?"

"Are there any openings?"

These were people I worked with, persons I knew outside of work, family, and even individuals at the church. They all had similar reactions.

Every single time I would have this conversation, I simply said, "I don't know if they are hiring or if any positions are available, but I know it is what I'm supposed to do." There wasn't a shred of doubt in me that I was making the wrong decision.

Now, yes, deciding to work for a church was rather a shock to me when I first realized that this might be what I do, especially when thinking back to a year prior and how far away from faith I was. However, after piecing back together various moments of my life, it didn't seem all that crazy or random. In fact, it seemed as if God had been formulating this path for me for years.

I remember when I was in around second grade, sitting next to my mom in church and telling her, "I think I want to be a priest." She looked at me with shock. "Why?"

I responded, "I think I could do it better than this guy" as I pointed up to the current priest with confidence in my voice.

She laughed and smiled at me, all followed by an encouraging nod.

Then there was the fact that I became an altar boy so I didn't have to just sit around at the church. This led to me loving being a part of the service. There were times in middle school where I really tried to get a hold of the whole faith thing with a burning passion. I was attending as many services as possible. Even in high school when I was attending confirmation classes for a short period of time, I always had a deep desire to discover what scripture was speaking to the world about.

I always had a desire to discover this whole faith thing. The problem was that I couldn't hold on long enough before I gained interest in something else or before I got too frustrated with how it was being presented to me.

Yes, this was a huge step, but I don't want anyone to think that it was an instant revelation or that there weren't little bread crumbs along the way that helped shape this decision. This is what I discovered during all of the reflection time over spring break.

So with the decision to work for the church being made, my next step was to figure out how. There weren't any applications online or links to apply. This didn't shock me due to the size of the church. They probably got thousands of requests a week from people wanting to work there. That's what made my friends laugh the hardest, in a loving way, about how confident I was that I was going to get a job there.

They would be like, "You have no ministry experience and no seminary schooling. You have only been an active follower of

Jesus for eight months at this point, and you are going to get a job there? Good luck!"

I knew they were just trying to be real and not get my hopes caught in some fantasy; however, none of those comments or truths fazed me. I knew this attempt was going to be something God wanted to teach me through figuring that He must have put this on my heart for a reason, whether I got the job or not.

With no idea how to apply, I did what only seemed logical at the time, but hilarious looking back now. I contacted HR and stated, "I would like a job. How do I apply?"

"Umm … well … we have a résumé submission link I can send you if you want," a lady said with the most confused expression in the tone of her voice. This might have been a request she didn't hear often, being in the HR department for the internal organization.

Confirming that I would like the link and confident as ever, I grabbed my laptop, ready to polish my résumé. After a few hours of work and some discussions with friends that I knew were really good with résumés, I opened up the résumé submission link. There were four questions to answer and a place to attach my résumé. I started to answer them even though it was getting late, thinking they wouldn't take long at all.

Four hours later, around two in the morning, I had finished the four "simple" questions and the résumé attachment. I wanted to make sure each word I put was perfectly placed, figuring this was the best shot I had at standing out among the rest. I went to bed with just a few hours of possible sleep available before having to get up to volunteer at the church that Sunday. Looking up at the ceiling, I said a little prayer, "All right, God. Here you go."

The next day, I was very tired from staying up so late. Also there was the fact that I could barely fall asleep, thinking about whether what I had said were the right things to say or not. I got ready and jumped in my truck to head to the church for my morning rehearsal.

On the drive there, I decided that I wouldn't go around and tell the world that I had applied at the church and beg for a job. No one ever gets a job when he or she seems desperate. Instead I decided I would only bring it up if it came up in natural conversation.

My time on stage had just finished up, and I was walking out of the room to get ready to head to the service that I attended when Erinleigh stopped me in the hall.

"Hey, is everything ok? I noticed you looked a little tired onstage," she stated.

"Yea, everything is fine. I didn't get much sleep last night," I replied.

"Oh, why not?" she asked.

"Well, I was up all night working on my résumé and filling out some job-related stuff," I stated, thinking back to my decision during the ride.

"Wait? Are you thinking about leaving teaching?" she asked with a very interested look, as she seemed laser focused on me now.

"I am leaving teaching. I told the school I will not be coming back next year, and I turned down my contract," I explained.

"Uh … where are you looking at working?" she asked, gaining more focus on what I was saying.

"Here actually. Last night I was up all night filling out the résumé submission form," I said with a huge smile on my face and a warm feeling filling my body, thinking how fast this conversation had already come up.

"Interesting," she said with a huge smile on her face. "That is good to know."

We left the conversation at that, as I walked away … well, skipped away.

A few weeks later, I received an email from Erinleigh asking if I were interested in coming in to have coffee with her to discuss some things. Instantly two very different thoughts entered my mind: *I'm fired from my volunteer position* or *She wants to talk about me applying to the church.* I'm still not too sure why I pondered the first thought. Nothing had been done that would have caused me to get let go as a volunteer, but you never know. Nothing lasts forever.

I showed up at the church about a week later to chat. She asked me various questions about why I was leaving my job, what led me to apply to work at the church, and what I was interested in doing at the church. One main thing we talked about was my desire for creating engaging environments. I went on explaining much of what I have already explained in this chapter to her.

Following all of my talking (which seemed like a lot more than usual), she calmly collected her thoughts as she thanked me for coming in. I said I'd love to interview if a job were available as we both began to walk out of the break room. She told me she would keep that in mind.

A few weeks went by before I heard anything back. Even though I didn't have a doubt that I was pursuing the right path, having the patience to discover where the path led was weighing on me.

Here is an excerpt of a journal entry I wrote during the time I was waiting to hear back that shows the struggle of patience.

*4/22/17*

*This time is hard. This is the ultimate test of faith. Everything I could possibly do to get a job at the church is done. Now I need to do the thing I struggle with the most, rely on God. I believe this is something I have grown in tremendously yet still have so much to go. My human nature and the comfortability of my old way of life is all too familiar, and often I find myself drawing back to that. I'm dead from that life, as Paul says in Romans. I need not even look back at what was as it is so opposite and different to what is.*

Shortly after that journal entry, Erinleigh confirmed that a position was available for me to interview for, and we began setting up times to do just that. I was going to be having a series of interviews that were to span over a few weeks, and following those interviews, I would know if more interviews were to take place.

One after another, I knocked out those interviews. Before I entered each one, I said the same little prayer that I had said before I went to bed that night after submitting my résumé, "All right, God. Here you go."

I said this prayer because it was all up to Him at this point. God had put the desire in my heart for ministry, but if I were meant for the specific job I was interviewing for, it would happen only through Him. I knew better than to think that, if I didn't get the job, God had failed me or let me down. That wasn't the point of any of this. The point was faith and trust in where He was leading me and what He was teaching me along the way.

Following the wave of interviews I did over the two weeks, I was contacted to move forward and have the final interviews for the position. After those, I was done. There were no more interviews. I was just waiting now. I just had to trust. I had to find the patience. I had to rely on faith.

At this point, it was the second-to-last week of the school year. I had been packing up my classroom in preparations for leaving the school and education all together. I was confident in the move I was making, but also terrified in how long it could be before I arrived at where God was leading me.

He led the Israelites through the wilderness for forty years before they were able to enter the Promised Land. That was where they were supposed to go, but it took a long time to get there. Was that going to be me? Was I going to be waiting for forty years before I discovered the ministry God was leading me to?

There was no guarantee after the interviews that I had the job. I knew I was still up against other candidates that, just like me, made it to the end of the interviews and were now waiting. Sitting in my classroom day after day on the second-to-last week, I'd be lying if I didn't doubt as time went on if it were all going to work out. That confidence I had slowly was starting to dwindle with every passing day.

Then my life changed forever. It was toward the end of the week, and I was heading to dinner with some friends. My phone rang, and I saw that it was Erinleigh.

*This could possibly be the call that tells me I didn't get it*, I thought to myself. My hands trembled as I picked up the phone.

After a few minutes of her explaining things, she said, "I would like to offer you the job. Do you accept?"

Tears started pouring down my face as I froze in my truck at the stoplight. I couldn't believe it. I was about to say the biggest yes I could have ever said.

"Yes! I accept!"

## From the Last Row

I could have very well ended this chapter and the book with that last story. I could have summed up that the last two months of my one full-year journey at the church were great and complete. However, God had one final thing to reveal that was the encore of all encores and brought my whole journey full circle from the beginning to the end.

It was Sunday night as I walked across the elementary ministry hallway, headed toward where the Sunday night gathering was going to be. This was a special night for the Sunday night gathering for a few reasons. Usually the gathering took place on the other side of the church; however, due to certain events and scheduling, the gathering moved locations to where it was going to be held that night. There were only two other times since I had been at the church that the gathering was in the current room. The first time was my first night there.

Another reason this was a special night for the gathering was that it was going to be the last time the gathering took place on Sunday night. In efforts to try out a new approach and to reach more people, the gathering was going to be moving to a weeknight.

There was one final reason, to me the most special reason, why this Sunday gathering was different from the other ones. This Sunday gathering was one year since I had walked into this building for the first time.

As I walked into the room on my way to where they were having the volunteer dinner before we went to serve, I reminisced on all that had happened over the year. I relived each story I shared in this book as I saw the original crew of people who helped make it all happen onstage, rehearsing for the night.

I looked down on the left side of my shirt. I saw one of the biggest ways that this year paid off. It was my badge that said "staff" on it with my name above it. I had entered the gathering as a nonbeliever and now was exiting this chapter of the gathering as a staff member of the very church that made it possible for me to truly and fully discover Jesus.

Saying hi to Mallory, I had an extra-excited tone in my voice. She asked me how I was doing as I said I was doing great. Then I went on to explain what was special about the night. She told me how amazing it all was as I headed back to eat.

After eating, Mallory pulled me aside and asked if I would share some words to the team before we all dismissed to go pull off the event. Completely shocked to get asked this, as not many people did, I stuttered to say sure and then asked what to say. She explained that I should share why this night was so special for me and how this gathering led to my current circumstances of being on staff. Feeling so honored, I accepted.

We all huddled together as I began to explain the specialty of the night. I explained what this gathering had done for me, how it created the place where I was finally able to experience the relationship with Jesus I was always meant to have, and how, because of that, I was able to find my truest calling of being in ministry. Warm smiles were seen all around the circle as you could see the inspiration for why we all did what we did to create this gathering sink in to each person. Mallory prayed for us, and we headed to our positions.

Under the "Come As You Are" banner as normal, I walked to my position and began interacting with those who were in the room already. Feeling completely fulfilled in life after getting to share my story to the people who had played such a huge part in it, I thought, *How could this night get any better?*

"Hey, Philip, could I talk to you for a sec?" Mallory asked as she pulled me aside from where I was standing minutes before the service was going to start.

"Sure, what's up?" I asked through the smile that wasn't able to leave my face.

"Hey, I was thinking. Do you want to come up onstage toward the end of the service and share your story?" she asked.

"Uh … Yea! I'd love to!" I pretty much screamed out, holding back the tears as she pointed to where I would sit.

The seat happened to be right next to Clay. He was going to be speaking tonight, and now it turns out was going to be interviewing me on my story through faith. I took a seat and waited to be called up.

As I walked up the steps, hearing my name called and friends in the crowd cheering since they had no idea I would be speaking, I was thinking about how amazing all of this was. Most importantly, how great God is to have turned my life into this.

Clay asked the first question about how I got to the church as I pointed to that last seat in the last row where I first sat and explained the rest of my story. The final question asked was where I was at that moment in my life. I got to share that now I was a staff member of the church in the elementary ministry, where I found some of my truest experiences with community that all started at the gathering. Applause filled the room, followed by Clay's prayer as we both walked off the stage and as the season of the Sunday night gathering and my first year at the church came to a close.

## Words for Thought

*Decisions*

Everything we do in life, every action causes a reaction. Whether it is something small like throwing a pebble in a pond and watching the ripples bump up against the shore or something big like saying "I do" and watching an entire family of generations form and impact the world, each decision results in something.

When looking at our decisions like that, it can almost be overwhelming. It can make us not want to take a step forward without weighing every single option, and it could leave us always planning but never actually doing. However, we cannot always plan, and we cannot always see every outcome. What will be in a month, a year, or ten years isn't always definite based on what we decide, but we still must decide. We must determine our next move, our next step, and our next interaction because the future is always becoming the present, and then it is our past.

We simply have to accept that we aren't always going to make the right decision, we aren't going to please everyone, and we aren't going to know what to do, but we still must do. Accepting these challenges will always propel us forward and keep us from getting stagnant in life.

My counselor has told me time and time again as I reflect on the decisions I have made that I have to trust that I did the best I could with what I knew at that moment. This has never made decisions easier, but it has helped me constantly move forward and not always dwell on what has passed and the impact it has made.

Throughout my year journey, I had to make a lot of decisions. The first time entering the building, choosing to volunteer, and deciding to invest in others, each and every decision had to be made. When I look back to where these decisions led, it can be easy to be tricked into thinking that I had a plan, I knew what would happen, and the outcome was guaranteed. As truthful as I can possibly be, I never, not once, had any idea what I was doing, what I really was committing to, and how it would play out one second later, let alone one year later.

Like I stated in the prologue, I simply said yes. I said yes to everything and decided I would ask questions later. I took chance after chance and hoped it turned out all right. I didn't have anything to lose because at the time it seemed as if I had nothing. It was decision after decision that sparked the "ready, fire, aim" mentality. One after another, I just kept saying yes.

If you find yourself stuck in life and not able to progress forward, I hope some things in this chapter were helpful. If you have been searching for your true calling, I hope that you continue to pursue it until you find it. One of the ways you might be able to find it is by volunteering.

*Volunteering*

There are so many things out there that are bigger than us. I'm not talking about physical things like buildings and bears, even though that is accurate. I am talking about movements and causes. Each day, we wake up and serve one of two causes: ourselves or others.

We need to assess if we have us or others in mind when we are going about our lives. Depending on the answer can depend on what we are getting out of life. Oftentimes it seems that those who are only serving themselves don't get much out of life. This book has been about finding sustainable joy, and serving yourself simply doesn't bring that.

If you want to truly find sustainable joy, serving others is one of the best ways to do it. When you see the impact your life has on others, it is as if your heart is being warmed by the hugs of each and every person you serve. It doesn't matter in what way you are serving others as long as you are serving others.

I happened to experience this joy while volunteering in the church. Through the elementary, high ministry, and Sunday night gathering environments, I was able to see how my life had a purpose and a reason for existence. Each and every interaction I had where I was for others and not wanting things from them, I could see the impact it was having on their lives. In return, sustainable joy in my own life started to form.

The church doesn't have to be the place you serve. I know tons of people who attend church that don't volunteer. That is ok. Maybe you don't attend church and aren't planning on it. First off, if you have made it this far in the book and that is you, thank you! Second, there are a million things you can do to serve others. The simplest way to find out how is to discover what you are passionate about.

If you like hosting, cooking, or really just food in general, maybe you can go to a local soup kitchen and volunteer. If you are really into technology, maybe you can go and volunteer to help teach kids coding. If you are really passionate about animals, you can possibly volunteer at the local animal shelter, playing with all the cute pups. Whatever it is that you are passionate about, there is something you can volunteer your services for.

Now I am not saying that you have to do this every day or even every week. I once read about a guy who goes to the local retirement home once a month and asks which resident gets the least amount of visitors. Once they give him a name, he spends the day with that person. I'm not even sure if he is passionate about the elderly, but he finds sustainable joy in doing it. So he continues.

At the church I work at, there is one day a year where all the staff are given various projects to go out and serve the community.

Even though it is just one day, the joy that comes from it is sustainable enough to last until the next year. What you are volunteering for can be every day, once a week, once a month, or even once a year. I promise the sustainable joy will come from it. What also can come from it is the discovery of a path in life that you were always meant to be on.

*Paths*

The common sequence of events following college is usually searching for any and every job. Whatever you find, accept it. That is at least the mentality my family instilled in me. If you were raised like me, then you know what I am talking about. It didn't matter if you liked your job or not. It was a job that paid the bills. Accept it!

Oftentimes, there are other results from accepting the first job that comes our way that aren't as beneficial as paying the bills. One of the results can be dreading going to work. If you are not passionate about your job and feel you weren't called to that position, it can become a coffin you sleep in every day. There is no motivation to work your hardest, no joy in what you do, and every excuse to get out as quick as possible.

Yes, there is the motivation of more money and higher status, but I promise you that those aren't sustainable joys, no matter who you are. A favorite quote of mine is from Jim Carrey, and it states, "I think everybody should get rich and famous and do everything they ever dreamed of so they can see that it's not the answer." There is so much truth in that quote that a whole book can be written about it.

Doing what you are doing simply for status, pay, or fame will never be the thing that keeps you satisfied and filled with joy. What does result from this is the mentality of "living for the weekend." To me, that is the worst mind-set there is. You work for five days and have the weekend for two days. I don't know how good you are at math, but about 70 percent of your days are spent working with that model. I don't want to dread 70 percent of my days and only hope for the 30 percent to be enough to bring me joy.

That was the realization I started to have when it came to teaching. It wasn't that I was dreading what I was doing; however, I no longer understood why I was doing it. The passion had diminished, and I was simply collecting a paycheck and hoping my weekends would keep me satisfied. I eventually got sick of that and decided to start searching for something that was going to bring me the joy I desperately needed.

Through discovering what you are passionate about and possibly serving others, you too might just find that employment elsewhere is the best thing for you. If your job is not leading you to the path you want to be on or is leading you to a path you don't want, why are you in that job?

Now, I am not saying that, if you are unhappy with your job, quit your job. What I am saying is, if you aren't passionate about your work, you need to discover what you are passionate about and pursue that. Maybe the job you are in will lead you to the path you want to head down but you haven't discovered how you can be passionate about your work yet. Perhaps the job you are in won't lead you down the path you want to head, but that job leads to another one that does. If this is the case, patience is the biggest thing in your current circumstances that you need.

*Patience*

The path we are meant to head down in life can and usually does take some time to form. Moses was in the wilderness for forty years before he was called to lead his people out of slavery.

Growing patience as your path is formed before you will be the single-most beneficial thing you can do.

As I sat waiting to see if I would get hired at the church, my patience was tested. I had to come to the realization that this job I was interviewing for might not be the job I was led to have in ministry. I had to cling to the hope and faith that I was heading down the right path, realizing it might take some time. In doing this, I had to prepare myself to be jobless for a certain amount of time, relying on the savings I had put aside to see where my path led.

Maybe patience for the right job is not what you need to develop. It could be that you have to develop patience for the right person to come into your life. As all those around you find their other half, get married, and have babies, you might be wondering when it is your turn. If that is you, I am right there with you.

For so long, I desperately searched to find the woman for me. Eventually I had this realization that God had the power to put the woman of my dreams in front of me at this very moment. The fact that He wasn't or at least that I couldn't see that He was could be that He is pointing me to something else right now. He very well could be trying to instill patience in me so that, when she does come along, it is perfect.

If you put all the ingredients to make a cake in a bowl, place it in the oven, and then pull it out before the timer goes off, you can eat it. However, it might make you sick or not be as good as if you waited. The same is true with whatever we have to be patient for. We need to know and trust that our path will lead us ultimately to where we were meant to be. I hope that your path eventually leads you to find sustainable joy.

*Challenge*

Through the various decisions you will have to make going forward from this point in your life, I hope and pray that they be prosperous ones. I hope that you see the impact simply saying yes can have on your life and that each decision is tied together somehow.

I challenge you to ask yourself if you are waking up to serve you or others. A friend of mine was chatting with me about this very thing. She said that it's all good and well to serve others, but she can just as well say she doesn't want to. I told her that she was correct; however, with a mind-set to only serve yourself, you might find that people don't want to be around you much longer.

It may seem harsh, but it is true. People want to know that you are for them and that you don't want something from them. Discover what you are passionate about and go out and volunteer your time. Doing that might just give you the purpose you have longed for in life and could lead you down a path you didn't know was for you.

As you head down whatever path in life, always remember to grow your patience. Like a cake, great things take time. The patience you need for whatever you are seeking might only be for a few days, or it can be for your entire life. That is what those who follow Jesus have to cling to. They accept Him and love Him for what He has done for them, but they have to wait until their lives here are over to actually see Him. That is the ultimate patience.

# EPILOGUE

There it is. That is my story, the tale of a nonbeliever walking into a church, giving it one last shot, saying yes to everything, and walking out a year later as a staff member of that very church with a life changed and fully devoted to Jesus. In one complete year through the power of God, I went from the last seat in the last row to the front of the room. I had found my sustainable joy.

Thank you so much for following my journey of finding what I was always after in the one place I never wanted to return to. My hope for this book was to give insight into how someone's life could be affected by walking into the local church and simply saying yes. Along with that, I wanted to pinpoint some things that can help contribute to sustainable joy in one's life.

The theme behind choosing to highlight saying yes so much in this book is a result from dwelling on how often we say no in life to the things that could benefit us the most. People are more overworked and sleep deprived than ever in today's society. We actually value being busy. However, all the things we constantly say yes to are usually things that can't provide us with that sustainable joy. The things most often said no to, like faith and the local church, are some of the things that can provide all we are truly looking for.

Now I am not oblivious. I understand the reputation that the church has in today's society. So often, news stories are displayed highlighting controversies and injustices that people carry out with the Bible and God as the forefronts of their false justifications. People are living every day with the wounds and scars of the experiences that they have had dealing with Christians, the church, and the assumptions they have about God.

It's easy to understand how so many can turn away from faith when being judged, labeled, or told that their lifestyle choices are wrong. If a stranger came up to me with those approaches, working in ministry or not, I would have a very hard time not being turned away from whatever they were trying to preach.

The biggest problem with faith and the church has never been faith or even God. It always stems back to how faith was explained, how the church was carried out, and how people put things in the way of the authentic message that Jesus teaches. When you peel back the layers of scripture and reveal the original intent of the local church, many would be surprised with how simple it is supposed to be and how freeing, welcoming, and loving it should be. Regardless, people have experienced so much wrong and disappointment in their experiences that they are done giving faith a try and would never walk back into a church.

Knowing that so many people could find what they are seeking if they would just step into the local church that truly was carrying out the message of Jesus and say yes, I decided to write this book. I decided to take all the risks, experiences, and outcomes from my journey walking back into the church one last time and compile them for others to see for themselves. My hope is that someone will read these stories, much like someone would read the reviews of a restaurant before actually going. And based on what they read, they would decide to give faith and the church one more try.

My book was always intended to give the most accurate and real accounts of what my experience was like. That was one of the reasons I wrote it right after all of these stories took place. It was also one of the reasons I shared certain parts to stories that didn't quite pan out miraculously or with a fairy-tale ending like Fefe's baptism. In the spirit of all of that, I don't want anyone to be misled that everything was glamorous on my journey.

Although this book highlights many wonderful things that came from the decisions to constantly say yes while attending a church for a year, not all had such easy consequences. Just like a social media picture that seems perfect, there are always triple the amount of less attractive ones.

There were times in my journey where I had to really stand in trust and test how much I believed all of it to be true when I ran into very strong differing opinions from people who were the closest to me. Some of these people cut me off from their lives temporarily and others permanently for what I believed and how I was going about expressing it.

I was told some of the most hurtful things imaginable from some of the people who were supposed to love me unconditionally. However, I knew what I was doing was the right thing to do and exactly what I was supposed to be doing.

Here is a part of a journal entry prayer highlighting this struggle I made during one of the hardest times of that year.

*11/8/16*

*Heavenly Father, I stood up about my beliefs. It was tough to do, as I always want to please, but I know that you, my heavenly Father, spoke to me and urged me to do it. I pray Lord that, when situations like this come up, which they will, where my faith and beliefs and how I am choosing to live my life are being challenged by others, especially those most dearest to me, you will give me the strength, Lord, to hold true and firm. I pray that I will not sell my faith short, I will not hide it, and I will not be affected by the viewpoints of others, but most importantly, I will be compassionate to them. I am your servant, and you are my master. Help me to never hide my master from the world. Amen.*

Saying yes to just about everything doesn't come without setbacks and downfalls. Because I was saying yes to everything, I ultimately got burned out in life for a season. With my commitments adding up to thirty-seven hours of a twenty-four-hour day, my overall health risks went up. All of the things I was a part of were so amazing and created some of the greatest stories in this book, but I learned that doing all of those things at one time was due to a lack of boundaries and balance on my part.

Here is an excerpt of a journal entry where I aired out the full intensity of that burned-out feeling at the time it was all happening.

*3/19/17*

*I feel so beat down, exhausted, and feeling like I need something to change. I feel physically, spiritually, emotionally, and mentally exhausted. I have never been this beaten down before. People can see it in my eyes and what I do, and they can hear it in my voice. I can't seem to make it go away.*

The burnout eventually led me to having to put a lot of things like coaching and some commitments outside of the church on hold for a while just so I could recuperate. My suggestion to anyone considering a season of saying yes is to obviously say yes with guidelines, boundaries, and balance so you are not overworked and run into any health risks.

One major thing in the book that I tried my very best to highlight and can't be missed was the element of time. It is truly amazing how all of these stories were able to take place or finish up within a year at the church; however, all took time to formulate. God isn't a genie, like I have said before. We can't wish things and miraculously have them happen.

It was a horrible series of years accompanied by a major health scare before I discovered the power of prayer. There were months of continuous waiting, silence, and doubt before I was able to interview for the job position at the church. Two decades of despicable life choices and bad experiences happened before I was able to fully see the power and glory that is God. It all took time.

Here is an excerpt from a journal entry I wrote around the time I was pursuing a job at the church, explaining the frustration of time.

*4/4/17*

*Why does time seem to stand still when waiting on something? Better yet, why do I anxiously beg for time to speed up? It is almost like I have the mind-set that God is great, but He would be a lot better if "this" happened or "this" stopped. Will I ever be content with all the undeserved things God has provided me? Will I find rest in knowing that I am not fighting against the clock? God has provided all the time I need and then has provided me eternity.*

I don't want any of this to diminish the power of the stories and experiences I had, let alone turn away anyone from considering the church. I just want to uphold my promise of being as accurate and honest about my journey so it is not another Christian story of miracle upon miracle without a hindrance of struggle along the way. If those exist in reality, that's awesome. It just didn't happen here.

## What Now

So what now? What do you do now that you have read all of this? You have heard the stories, lived through the experiences from my perspective, and given insight into the possibilities of finding sustainable joy that could be. Well, the easiest thing to say is "go find a church." However, I know this might not be the present reality for all who read this book. It would be naïve of me to think that every person who reads this book, after hearing about my experiences, would be convinced to throw away all of his or her struggles with faith and the church and just hop right in.

For those who did have that experience with this book, I am so grateful that my stories were able to provide a little guidance on the beautiful journey that God has laid out for you. I am praying every day that your life experiences would be just as fruitful if not more than mine were and continues to be. Please don't be discouraged if you walk into a church tomorrow and don't have the same experience or still feel emptiness inside. It takes time, trust, and, most importantly, Jesus.

My hope is that the church you do walk into is one that captures Jesus's true message and the intentions of the original church, but if it isn't, don't give up. There are so many churches out there. Maybe one day we will get to sit next to each other in the second row and worship together. That would be incredible!

For the people reading this book who already are invested in the local church and taking steps in your faith, my hopes and prayers are that, through my stories, you are able to see the power and impact you have on other's lives who might not be at the current state you are in. I hope you are encouraged and inspired to invite people to the second row with you, to connect with those deeper that you are serving with, and to not put obstacles in the way of those who are trying to discover faith that have been put in front of them before.

Along with this, I hope you are inspired to never give up on your faith and the power that the local church can have on so many others with your involvement. Continue to search for ways to provide sustainable joy in your life and the lives around you. Share your experiences with others and the stories you have lived. Don't ever think that you don't have the power to impact someone's life.

All my life, I was always labeled as a storyteller, and in most contexts, it wasn't ever said in a positive sense. Through the stories I've lived and now those that I have told, that storyteller label can be used in the most positive sense to help anyone who might need it.

My campus pastor said this to my volunteers one night before our afternoon service that I think resonates so much to this point. He said, "We are not just affecting a thousand lives, but instead we are affecting a thousand lifetimes." Each and every person that you interact with in and out of the church has a life where he or she will interact with thousands of other people and the lives those people will interact with.

Your story is so special. Don't ever let people stop you from sharing it or living it. You never know whom the thousands of lifetimes are that you will affect.

Now for those of you who aren't there and wouldn't say you're ready to walk into a church yet. The first thing I will say is that there are thousands of churches that stream online content that you can access if you want to take a small step forward before the giant step of walking into the physical building. However, maybe you aren't ready or don't want to give faith a try at all. That is ok!

My hope for you through my stories is that you walk away knowing that you are not alone. There might be loneliness present in your life, but hopefully now you are left with some great ways to build a healthy community around you. Maybe volunteering for the church isn't up you alley and your friends would never do that. That's ok. Find something that you or your friends are passionate about—a movement, a cause, or an organization—and volunteer for it. You might be surprised at what it will do for your life and your feeling of purpose.

My hope for you through my stories is that you see the possibilities of trying something, healthy, that is, that you have always said no to. It could be something that changes your life forever. Maybe just this one time, say yes to it.

Go on the vacation you have been putting off for years. Contact the friend who wronged you that you have refused to talk to for months. Leave the job that has grown as a safety net

161

for you but you don't enjoy, and take the risk of chasing after a passion that weighs deeply on your heart.

I'm not saying for anyone that you will have the same experiences I had in the church or that taking the risks I did will pan out like mine. All I'm trying to point out are the possibilities that can be created by changing your normal course of action, approaching situations like you have never done before, and simply saying yes to things you have always said no to. Through these, whether it's from the local church or not, you just might find the sustainable joy you have always searched for.

I want to leave you all with one final quote that sums up this whole book and was an encouraging hope for me through this entire journey. This quote was stated by Brian Houston, the pastor of Hillsong Church from the *Hillsong* movie, and it says, "Find a local church, pour your life into it, and it'll never be the same again."

Now it's your turn. Ready, fire, aim!

# ACKNOWLEDGMENTS

The main and first one I must thank is God. Lord, you are truly amazing in all the wonder that is you. From the time before I was born to the time after I am long gone from this earth, you have seen it all. Without you, I wouldn't be alive right now. I am forever grateful you sent your Son Jesus to pay for my sins so I could have a relationship with you now and forever. God, thank you for guiding me to your church, providing me with the experiences of a lifetime, and encouraging me to write this book. I lift up this book and all the stories in it to you.

Now there are so many people who have made such huge impacts throughout my life and my journey at the church and during the process of writing this book. I know for a fact I won't be able to name each and every single person who has helped, guided, and shaped me along the way in my life. With this in mind, I want to thank everyone.

If you have read this book and feel you have played some role in the formation of these stories or the development of my life, I sincerely, from the bottom of my heart, thank you. Without you, none of this would have been possible. I'd be more than happy to provide a personal thank you to you if you reach out and contact me.

David, thank you so much for always taking the time to sit and talk with me about faith, confusions I have, counsel I need, the struggles that weigh on me, and everyday life. I am so truly blessed to have met you and have you in my life in such a pinnacle role. As I have told you time and time again, this book could be titled *Philip and David's Adventures* because you have played such a prominent role in my first year at the church and continue to play to this day.

Heather, words are hard to describe as to the impact you have made in my life. Without you reaching out to help a new friend at the school, none of these stories would have ever happened. I cannot thank you enough. I'm so glad our friendship has grown, and I will never forget all the conversations we have had during the first year as I truly discovered a faith of my own. My life has literally changed because of your friendship.

Ashley and Micah, thank you so much for the endless roles you play in my life. From the times we were in college and you saw the lost soul in me who needed desperate help to the entire process of me writing this book, you both have never given up on me regardless of my behavior and have always provided never-ending support through my journey. You two fully encapsulate what it means to disciple another person through the power and love of Jesus. So much of the words written in this book had you both in mind as I reflected on our lives together, the roads we traveled, and the stories we shared. Thank you so much for continuing to be my cheerleaders and encouragers through all the struggles of writing this book.

Josh, your friendship is without a doubt one of the most genuine things I have in my life. Thank you so much for your wisdom and passion for Jesus that you share with me each and every day. Thank you for teaching me what it truly means to be vulnerable and fully known by few. Your feedback and support through this entire writing process has made it possible for me to finish this book.

Mallory and Adam, thank you so much for seeing the need to connect people to community and creating the Sunday night gatherings. You created an environment where a lost soul like myself could walk in and instantly be loved and accepted. You both fully live a ministry life of allowing people to come as they are, just like the banner that hung above my head night after night. Without you two, your loving hearts, and caring passion for other people's stories, my stories may have never been shared or even existed.

Adam and Heather, thank you for always being the warm and welcoming hug I need. Because of you two allowing me into your lives, I learned what it meant to allow others into mine. You both showed me the passion and personal care it takes to fully serve high school students and what ministry is all about. Both of you were some of the first people I met at the church and helped to start the endless community that has formed around me to this day.

To Leigh Ann, thank you so much for always investing time in my life during some of my toughest days. Thank you for being one of the first to show me what faith and a relationship with God could actually look like if I were to just give it a chance. You and your family were with me every step of the way through every setback and discovery, which helped form the building blocks of me discovering Jesus. Thank you for so many years of friendship during our childhood that helped me to flourish into adulthood.

Ron, thank you for your mentoring that is always there when I need it most. Thank you for taking the time out of your life to invest in someone like me. You have personally guided me through so many misconceptions and struggles of faith and trust that have helped make all of this possible. You are the example of what it looks like to invest in the next generation and are a huge role model for me as I move toward my future.

My small group consisting of Josh, Tommy, Grayson, Nick, Vince, Marcus, Gabe, and Ryan, thank you so much for being my support system, my accountability group, and, most of all, my truest of friends. We have shared so much together, and you all have been there for me every step of the way through all of my struggles. Without you guys, I would have never had the courage to be vulnerable and real in this book.

Mom, thank you for always being the pillar of faith in my life. Regardless of the seasons we were in or what the circumstances were, you always stood strong in your faith in God. You have provided a life for me that makes me proud to wake up every single day and show it off to the world. From the times you held me when I cried to the hugs you gave me when I celebrated, you have fully encompassed what a parent should be to a child. There are so many memories we have shared, so many tough paths we have went down together, and so much hope we live for now that all are displayed on the heart sign I made you for at Christmas that hangs on your wall. Every day that I get to share the love of Jesus with others, I do because you helped give me life and a reason to live. Thank you!

Dad, not a day goes by where you are not on my mind and heart. I know you are up in heaven right now, and through the entire process of me writing this book, you are smiling down upon me. You showed me twenty-five years of glorious life. Your sense of humor and your laugh will always be heard in my ears. Thank you for showing me how much fun moments of life can be with a little change of perspective. Thank you for the never-ending care you always provided me as I grew up, regardless of whether I wanted it or not. Thank you for teaching me hard work and giving my best effort, two qualities that this book couldn't have been written without. I can't wait till we see each other again in heaven. Thank you for the life we had together.

Erinleigh, thank you for believing and investing in me because you saw things others didn't. Your guidance, passion, and empathy you pour out every day inspires me more and more to give my full life to ministry. Thank you for investing day after day in me so I can grow and become the best of who I am meant to be professionally, personally, and spiritually.

My counselor, thank you so much for meeting with me week after week to work through some of the hardest things my life has experienced. The things you have helped me uncover, the insight you have provided, and the genuine care you have displayed has not only kept my life going in the fallout of a tragedy but has helped my life become better than I could have ever imagined.

My team at the church, thanks for always being a support system that I can rely on. You all have welcomed me with open arms, helped me in times of need, and continue to provide care for my family in the toughest times. Like my mom has said to me time and time again, we would have never made it through the death of my dad without you all. Thank you so much for giving my family hope and giving me life each and every day. You all collectively demonstrate what a love and passion for other people getting to experience the love and passion of Jesus looks like.

My church and the Sunday night gathering, this book is my thank you note to you. Thank you so much for your passion to reach those who don't attend church. This book is a direct example of what happens every single day throughout your halls and endless lives of people you reach. Because of the environments you create and the people you invest in, there are people like me who get to have the fog removed from their lives so they can see the beauty God has created for them. Without you all, I probably wouldn't be alive right now to write all of this. You have become my home here that I never want to leave.

To James, thank you for being the inspiration for the title of this book. We have so many hilarious memories and stories that perfectly display a "ready, fire, aim" mentality. Thank you for a friendship that will never expire no matter where life takes us. Thank you for the endless laughs we have shared together and being a guiding voice for me through my college years.

Dave, Keith, Mitch, Josh, and Anna, thank you so much for helping edit the original copy of my book. Your feedback and suggestions took this book to a level I could have never imagined. The honesty you all provided, although not easy to do, was done with the fullness of your hearts and the genuine care for mine. May the words printed on these pages be infused with the love and wisdom you have provided.

To WestBow Press, thank you so much for the hours and hours you all have put into making this book possible. Thank you for taking the risk on me after hearing the pitch for my book and believing in my stories as much as I do. You all have made it possible so my stories reach thousands and thousands of people all around the world. You all have made it possible for people to walk back into the local church and give it another try, which could possibly change the course of their lives forever. Thank you for being a platform God can use so authors like myself can share God's message and amazing works.

To all the endless stories that took place throughout my life and my first year at the church that didn't make it into this book, thank you. You were millions of small parts that created the big picture of my life and my journey. The people I interacted with, the smiles and laughs shared, and the tears shed were all part of a bigger plan.

All the readers of this book, thank you for taking a chance on my life and me, like all the people throughout my stories. You all are my truest inspiration and whom I pray for every single day. Through the endless hours up late writing to the times where writer's block took over, I always was able to push on because of you all. Thank you for reading this book, especially all the way to the end, and coming along through the journey of my life.

Finally to those who might feel lost, be struggling, be barely holding on or not wanting to much longer, or wanted to put down this book time and time again, thank you for holding on. Thank you for sticking with me. Thank you for stepping out in faith when so much is trying to push you down. My hope is you find the peace you are looking for in this life and maybe, just maybe, it happens to be from a church you decide to attend as you discover the God who loves you exactly where you are and is waiting for you with His arms stretched out wide open to hold on to you and never let go. May you find sustainable joy.

To everyone, thank you!

CPSIA information can be obtained
at www.ICGtesting.com
Printed in the USA
BVHW071408150119
537889BV00001B/34/P

9 781973 648512